Marriagebrokers

A Rational Look at Marriage in Today's Society

by
Charles Stephen Fossett, III

authorHOUSE

AuthorHouse™
1663 Liberty Drive, Suite 200
Bloomington, IN 47403
www.authorhouse.com
Phone: 1-800-839-8640

© 2008 Charles Stephen Fossett, III. All rights reserved.

No part of this book may be reproduced, stored in a retrieval system, or transmitted by any means without the written permission of the author.

First published by AuthorHouse   1/21/2008

ISBN: 978-1-4343-0892-4 (sc)

Library of Congress Control Number: 2007907060

Printed in the United States of America
Bloomington, Indiana

This book is printed on acid-free paper.

For "Mommy"
December 30, 1931- May 3, 2007

Also by Charles Stephen Fossett, III

───────────

Heartbrokers: A Rational Look at Romantic Love and Relationships

"To be nobody but yourself—in a world which is doing its best, night and day, to make you everybody else—means to fight the hardest battle which any man can fight, and never stop fighting."

E. E. Cummings

Contents

Preface
xiii

1
Marriage and the Wedding: *Forever and a Day*
1

2
Marriage and Forever: *'Til Death Do You Part*
9

3
Marriage and the NIKE™ Approach: *"Just Do It"*
17

4
Marriage and Religion: *The Religious Marriagebrokers*
21

5
Marriage and Expectations: *At Your Service*
29

6
Marriage and Power: *Heads or Tails?*
35

7
Marriage and Conflict: *Fight the Good Fight*
41

8
Marriage and Divorce: *When to Let Go*
55

9
Marriage and Me: *Me, Myself, and We*
61

10
Marriage or Me: *A Life Without Marriage*
67

11
Marriage and Tradition: *Some Creative Alternatives*
73

12
Marriage and the Future: *Is Marriage Obsolete?*
79

13
Epilogue: *A Final Word*
83

Notes
89

Illustrations

Figure 1	Linear Lifeline Continuum	12
Table 1	Biblical Characters and Marital Relationships	23
Figure 2	Greater Role Expectation Scale	30
Figure 3	Greater Personal Happiness Scale	32
Figure 4	Chivalry and Equality Scale	36
Table 2	Effects of Chivalry	38
Figure 5	Lower Conflict and Passivity Scale	44
Table 3	Relationship Power Strategies	45
Figure 6	Greater Passivity and Independence Scale	47
Figure 7	Lesser Independence and Low Self-esteem Scale	48
Figure 8	Low Self-esteem and Personal Happiness Scale	50
Figure 9	Greater Conflict and Passivity Scale	50
Figure 10	Lesser Passivity and Independence Scale	51
Figure 11	Greater Independence and Low Self-esteem Scale	51
Figure 12	Less Low Self-esteem and Personal Happiness Scale	52
Table 4	Pros and Cons of Creative Marriages	78

Preface

> "Human kind cannot bear much reality."
> T. S. Eliot

In my previous book, *Heartbrokers: A Rational Look at Romantic Love and Relationships*, I suggested that we should view our romantic relationships from a more rational perspective. Moreover, that we should merge the emotional and the logical as we can never fully eliminate our sentimental tendencies. I must confess, though, I was a little skeptical whether the combination of rational thought and emotional response was conceivable. However, after much consideration and after reading various writings on logical and critical thinking,[1] I am further convinced that rationality and sentiment may work together harmoniously to add stability and possibly longevity to romantic relationships.

Emotions are primarily physiological reactions to certain stimuli. Not much thought is involved or even necessary for emotions to surface. Additionally, responding emotionally, for the most part, is learned behavior. We know this because not everyone reacts identically to the same situations. Many societies teach their members to react or not to react differently to similar circumstances. What makes us angry, because of our social programming may have little or no affect on someone who has an entirely different upbringing. For example, in American culture we are preoccupied with the idea of time. We, subsequently, become annoyed when someone fails to arrive for an appointment promptly. Conversely, people in many South American countries do not stress punctuality. As a result, they may not react emotionally when someone arrives late. Their actions or inactions are, like ours, a direct result of their social programming.

Clearly, we find that although our feelings are an integral aspect of our human existence, various societies utilize and apply them differently. Still, I argue that these same learned attitudes and subsequent responses are what cause the breakdown of our intimate relationships. This, primarily, is because we often react instinctively to situations without the burden of logical thought or evaluation. Our sentiments, oddly enough, tend to justify our irrational behavior and therefore relieve us of the responsibility of assessing how they adversely affect our relationships with others. "You know I get emotional sometimes," we say.

Our emotional socialization, however, does not necessarily mean that we are irreversibly predestined to have our sentiments guide our actions. Unfortunately, we frequently respond unrealistically to certain situations. When I was 12 years old or so, whenever I got angry my mother used to tell me to count to ten before I responded to what others did. This practice, evidently, was to motivate me to think as opposed to just reacting. Usually, my emotionally motivated reactions got me into trouble and caused me considerable regret. On the other hand, when I actively thought about my conduct, I greatly moderated my behavior. Still today, more times than not, after thinking through a situation, I realize its pettiness.

Undoubtedly, we can successfully regulate emotionalism, but only with rationalism. Rational thinking restrains expressive actions. If we desire to cultivate and maintain a workable romantic and/or marital relationship, it is essential that we do not use our emotions as a crutch or as the foundation of our matrimonial decisions and behaviors. Emotions have a function in all of our personal interactions. They, undoubtedly help to promote and strengthen our social attachments. Left unchecked, however, emotionally charged romanticism might continue to generate conflict and uncertainty in our marriages as well as within our other intimate associations.

The marriagebrokers choose to ignore the profoundly negative affects our unbridled feelings and tendency for irrational decision-making have on our marriages. They, subsequently, encourage us to pay no heed to these influences. Marriagebrokers like all agents trying to get people to purchase their products or buy into their ideas, generally push the positive and downplay the negative. Brokers of all types go to extreme measures to distract potential customers from the obvious. Many times, they only reveal the downside of their products or concepts out of legal and not moral obligation. They commonly reserve this information to small, fine print at a particular spot at the end of the document or television commercial.

Notwithstanding, marriagebrokers are not regulated by government watchdogs. They are, consequently, free to barter away and manipulate our feelings and subsequently control our ideas about marriage for their financial and political gain. We, generally, do not question the motives or intentions of the marriagebrokers. We are comfortable with accepting their unregulated and unproven concepts as the truth and the only way of life.

Hence, I wrote this book to encourage you to consider the obvious. I hope that you will begin to see and even question the ideas that the marriagebrokers try so hard to hide from us. I know that your first instinct will be to doubt the theories that I present. This is both understandable and predictable. Indeed, if you also have the nerve to question the obvious, you will reap the social wrath of your family and peers. It takes a certain measure of courage or madness to withstand the ridicule that accompanies social defiance at any level. Even so, the resultant opposition may only strengthen you in the end. Nevertheless, if you push through the emotions that prevent rational analysis and consider my position, you will begin to realize that there is life before, during, and after the traditional marriage standard of living.

Marriage and the Wedding: *Forever and a Day*

"All weddings are similar, but every marriage is different."
John Berger

The wedding ritual is the one aspect of the marital process that receives the greatest attention in many societies. In American culture, future brides and grooms spend countless hours planning and organizing the special events of the day. For most potential mates, the wedding ceremony remains an important and the most visualized part of matrimony. Consequently, many of them, especially brides, make wedding preparations months or years in advance. At times adolescent girls have vivid notions of what they want their weddings to be like down to the colors of the bridesmaid's dresses. Others have a collection of brides magazines stashed in their closets or under their mattresses. Most would-be brides cannot or better yet, would not ever consider getting married without having an elaborate ceremony.

Future brides are as a rule overwhelmed with excitement after they officially announce their engagement. They immediately share the good news with their close friends and family who usually respond jubilantly. The future groom also tells his co-workers and acquaintances. They too typically share his enthusiasm. The parents react as though the proposed marriage represents a type of rite of passage where their child is finally taking the ultimate step towards adulthood.

Even those who are not participating in the festivities are equally as excited about the news of a wedding. They encourage the proposed pair to go all out on the ceremony. Family members also support the bride and groom's decisions by telling them that they only get married once so they should do everything to make the occasion a memorable one.

News of the wedding spreads like wildfire by everyone socially connected to the future couple. The only individuals who appear to receive the news with regret and remorse are the close friends of the groom—at least in the case of his single friends. For the most part, they invariably see the marriage of their friend as a loss.

After a while, verbally spreading the news becomes tiresome. Therefore, the bride usually orders custom designed invitations to help circulate the word. She dispatches them to friends and relatives all over the country and sometimes the world. As the date draws closer, money becomes less important than the blissful, dream-fulfilling event.

The bride and groom unknowingly test friendships as the hierarchy and order of appearance in the wedding company measure the validity of their long-term associations. Additionally, couples immediately contract individuals specializing in every aspect of the matrimonial process. These specialists call themselves professional wedding consultants. They often from the start plan to incorporate age-old traditions in the ceremony.

At some point before the wedding, the girls may arrange a bridal shower and a bachelorette's party for the future bride. They bombard her with numerous gifts at the shower. These gifts usually include sex toys and erotic lingerie (even though most of these gadgets and garments are doomed to dry rot in an obscure nightstand drawer in the uneventful years that follow the wedding). The bachelorette's party they throw typically involves plenty of shielding of the eyes and embarrassing squeals in the presence of the scantly clad professional entertainment—although there is as a rule one girl in the crowd aggressively groping the dampened thongs of the male erotic dancers.

The groom's friends also organize a party for him. The bachelor's party largely consists of beautiful professional, half-dressed strippers. This precious event is primarily to expose the future groom to the pleasures of life that he will never again experience without the threat of serious retaliation from his soon-to-be wife.

Finally, the greatly anticipated day arrives. People travel for miles in response to the wedding invitations. They do not arrive empty-handed, however. The guests bring with them as gifts all manner of practical household items. On the assigned table in the reception hall are neatly wrapped crock-pots, cheese servers, bathroom towels, face cloths, bed linen and all types of small appliances. Everyone gathers in the sanctuary adorned in their best attire and wait impatiently to witness the ceremony of completeness.

Symbols of solidarity saturate the sanctuary. When the ceremony begins, the bride and groom may each take a candle and simultaneously light a single, larger candle positioned at the front of the church. Some wedding customs have the couple attach a single piece of string to their wrists symbolizing the inseparable element of a life-long union. Still other rituals involve them jumping over a broom or crushing a wine glass under their feet in unison, or even drinking from the same goblet in chorus.

The dialogue of the officiator further expresses the idea of unity when they announce to the congregation, "…these two now have become one." Yet, the universal representation of cohesion remains the exchanging of the wedding bands. The rings supposedly symbolize the never-ending, unbroken bond that will exist between the husband and the wife. All of these traditions are significant in reinforcing the notion that two distinct individuals are now becoming a single unit.

They, additionally, verbally proclaim their eternal commitment to the sacred institution of marriage by answering, "I do" to the "death do you part" portion of the wedding vows. After performing these traditional customs, the bride and groom turn to the audience and publicly declare their undying devotion to the ideology of one. Finally, they conclude their public proclamations with the ultimate sealing of the deal in the form of a kiss. Their heroic actions meet with thunderous applause and the heart-felt praise of the onlookers. Tears flow freely. The newly joined couple gestures bows and waves to the endearing crowd as they proceed down the aisle—formally as two, but now as one.

The guests form greeting lines. They offer handshakes and generously shower upon the new couple congratulatory hugs and kisses. Everyone soon adjourns to the reception hall where they patiently wait while the bride and groom make a photographic history of the day's events.

The elated couple finally arrives at the reception hall. The guests anxiously wait in line for an opportunity to dance the wedded waltz with them. Family and friends are eager to stuff five, ten, and twenty dollar bills into the bride and groom's under garments. Everyone is thrilled and in a festive mood as they celebrate the bliss filled union of their loved ones. Musical tunes of matrimonial praise blare in the background. This oneness ceremony typically leads to a preplanned honeymoon excursion, generally, to a far off island that neither the bride nor groom will ever visit again.

Given all of the pomp and circumstance that surrounds the wedding ceremony, it is no wonder why many would-be spouses gleefully anticipate this brief and public event. However, what would be the implications if you planned a wedding and no one showed? What if you, as the bride or groom to be, told all of your friends that you were planning to get married and they wept out of disappointment and disbelief? What if nobody RSVP'd? What if everyone in your family and all of your closest friends tried to talk you out of it? Moreover, what if no one brought gifts, there were no parties, no dinners, no adulation, or no support? Would you still be just as eager to enter into such a life-long bond?

Further, consider what would happen if all of our social role expectations concerning marriage were twisted, and we viewed getting a divorce just as positively as getting married. Actually, when do you really need for all of your closest friends to gather in celebration on your behalf? When do you most need them to give you practical gifts like crock-pots, can openers, cheese servers, bath towels, and bed linen? When do you really need them to shower you with five, ten, and twenty dollar bills? When do you need their heart-felt adulation and undying support? When would all of these things benefit you the most than after a turbulent divorce where your spouse just took half of all your worldly possessions? Assuredly, the divorce rate in this country would skyrocket if everyone we knew reacted favorably to our decision to dissolve our marriage.

Hence, we see the primary function of the wedding ceremony. The marriage ritual remains a formal, positive sanction[2] that a particular society uses to manipulate the matrimonial attitudes, decisions, and behaviors of its members. Most individuals choose to conform to pre-established social guidelines of matrimony rather than suffer the public ridicule that accompanies remaining single or getting a divorce.

The splendor of the wedding ceremony tends to overshadow the actual marriage. This may explain why we spend far more time, energy, and rational thought planning and organizing the wedding than we do considering the dynamics of the marriage. We do not solicit premarital consultants as aggressively as we seek wedding planners and other experts. We pour more attention and thought into choosing dress styles and color coordination than we do investigating the details of an anticipated life-long union. We purchase bridal magazines and books and study them with determined intensity. We, therefore, thoroughly diagram and think through the wedding while paying close attention to every detail of the day's events. Weddings last for just one day. We expect marriage, however, to last a lifetime. Why then do we spend hundreds of hours and thousands of dollars on the temporary wedding ritual and very little time and money on the marriage? We, additionally, rarely take the time to read or research philosophical, sociological, or psychological materials concerning the dynamics associated with marriage.

Unfortunately, we leave the marital preparations unattended. We expect the marriage to develop with little or no input from our families, the so-called experts, or us. It is, indeed, considerably more sensible to focus on the long-term institution as opposed to the extremely short-lived formal procedure. Nevertheless, other members of our social circles often discourage and admonish us if we attempt to marry without having a formal and an elaborate celebration.

Over time, the media has severely commercialized marriage, particularly, the wedding ritual. The economic marriagebrokers have successfully diverted our focus from matrimony to the nuptials. They market every aspect of the wedding rite. The bridal business is a multi-billion dollar industry in the United States ($70 billion per year to be exact).[3] The standard couple spends, on the average, $20,000 on the ceremony alone. This is up from $4,000 in 1984.[4]

However, the economic marriagebrokers are not at all interested in long-term outcomes. In actuality, they may benefit more from divorce, as they will again reap substantial profits when people remarry. Their primary concern, however, is marketing to the public those products and ideas that will bring them revenue. Therefore, the economic marriagebrokers emphasize the tangible and deemphasize the nontangible and, arguably, the most important aspects of marriage. From a rational standpoint, the type of dress worn by the bride, the color of the tuxedo worn by the groom, the kind of venue where the wedding takes place, the number of guests that attend, the type of catering at the reception, etc. has little if nothing at all to do with marriage. All are simply moneymaking opportunities for the economic marriagebrokers. Clearly, and in their defense, it is not the ultimate responsibility of the economic marriagebrokers to investigate the workings of the marital institution. The burden of rational, premarital analysis remains solely with the soon-to-be couple.

Notwithstanding, potential brides and grooms are discouraged from taking a logical position when it comes to the wedding and the marriage. Traditionally, the love ideology is trusted to take care of the necessary particulars of wedlock. Nevertheless, potential partners must consider important factors. These factors include taking an honest and sensible look at why they decided to marry in the first place. Couples should address realistic economic goals. Additionally, they should think reasonably about what they will do if the union falters. Furthermore, they should reveal, analyze, and overly simplify their personal expectations of the relationship.[5] Before the vows, couples should determine whether their marital expectations are more important than their spouse is. Honest evaluation of their basic motivation to marry may lead to outcomes that are more desirable. Marital romanticism may then give way to marital rationalism.

What I have found astounding is the lack of mental premarital programming. It is as if we deem the institution of marriage so natural a process that we take it for granted. However, a critical look at the excessively high divorce rate in this country proves the contrary. Marriage is not a natural development. Divorce, however, may be. To prove my point, I suggest you try this experiment the next time someone tells you that he or she has set a date to get married. Ask them how many articles or books they have read or how much research about marriage and divorce statistics they have undertaken (brides' magazines, books, and other commercial literature are not valid sources). Try to resist the initial urge to offer the typical congratulatory reinforcement. Further, ask them whether they have consulted a non-biased premarital counselor. This means professional, learned consultants, not poorly trained, non-professionals or religious marriagebrokers.[6] These types of non-professional counselors include people like your local pastor or priest—most of whom have no formal marital relationship counseling, education or training. They, nevertheless, have considerable input and extensive influence on individual attitudes and expectations of marriage.[7] Unfortunately, the extent of their premarital counseling is generally limited to a brief and informal counseling session just prior to the wedding.

Further, ask the excited future couple to compare the amount of time they plan to spend on wedding preparations with the amount of time they plan to spend on marriage preparations. You will find that there will be a substantial inconsistency between the two. There is further emphasis of this inconsistency when we appraise the amount of money invested in the wedding against the amount of money devoted to the marriage. Again, the time and money exhausted on the wedding is far more than what is spent on the most important aspect of a union—the marriage.

I should clarify that I am not suggesting that we totally abandon the greatly hyped nuptial festivities. Wedding ceremonies, I believe, have a distinct, socially binding function in all societies. However, I am challenging potential spouses to strike a balance between economic and rational wedding and marriage preparations.

A critical look at the matrimonial ritual leads us to believe that weddings benefit everyone except the bride and groom. Similarly, funerals do not edify the deceased, but serve merely to solidify and reinforce the social bond between the living.[8] Henceforth, we do not gear weddings toward adding strength to the bride and groom's relationship.

It appears that the marital custom is specifically a social instrument used to satisfy the public's question of morality between individuals involved in a sexual relationship. Subsequently, marriage is the means whereby couples who are sexually attracted to one another can legitimately satisfy their natural urges without negative social consequence. Hence, the marriage ceremony symbolizes social conformance to pre-established norms. After the ceremony, however, everyone retreats to his or her own social habitat and leave the new couple alone to decipher the marital code.

What baffles me out of all of the things I have stated, is that there is no solid evidence whatsoever that supports the fact that the more time and money we spend preparing for the wedding the greater the guarantee of the longevity of the union. Unfortunately, many times the excitement of the wedding ceremony outlasts the enthusiasm for the marriage in that long after the vows are declared couples still never realize genuine happiness.

Our obsession with the ritual may explain why many of us go through with the marriage even though we know we are making a big mistake. If only we can become as enchanted with the institution of marriage as we are with the wedding. It is essential that we begin to see weddings for what they are. Again, weddings serve a particular social function. They make it easier for us to bring our lives in line with what society expects of us. Still, they are social functions that we should rationally evaluate if we expect longevity and personal fulfillment from our relationships. The marriagebrokers, however, discourage us from critically assessing this portion of the marriage process. This is irrational. Weddings are joyful events that everyone in attendance should enjoy—considering the amount of money spent. Nevertheless, I cannot emphasize enough how we can ill afford to expect a fleeting social ritual to be the instrument that springboards our marriages into happiness and success.

Marriage and Forever: 'Til Death Do You Part

"The dread of loneliness is greater than the fear of bondage, so we get married."
Cyril Connolly

One of the most profound oaths echoed at wedding ceremonies is the proclamation, "...until death do you part." Practically every bride and groom enters into their marriage with the gleeful hope that their love, passion, and their marriage will endure despite the obstacles they encounter over the term of their union. This optimism persists even in the face of concrete evidence that many marriages are doomed to fail within the first 10 years.[9] The marriagebrokers insist that every couple should strive to attain the ultimate goal of marital longevity, nonetheless.

In lieu of the present evidence that tends to nullify the high expectation of wedded durability, the hope of cohabitating with a single mate for an extended period seems pointless. Still, our aspirations of permanence thrive. However, let us consider this *forever* notion more critically. After I publicly swear my allegiance to my wife, for the next fifty years—or the rest of my life, which ever comes first—I am, in essence, bound by secular and moral law to have no other sexual contact with another human being other than her. In some instances, the depth of a couple's commitment is even greater when they believe that cheating and other forms of infidelity does not even involve having physical or sexual contact with someone else. Infidelity, in their minds, encompasses mental or emotional straying away from the relationship. In other words, if you think about being with someone other than your lover or spouse, or if you are attracted to someone, you have still cheated. This is true even though you have never actually acted upon your emotional impulses. If we take these parameters of faithfulness into consideration, it becomes relatively impossible to ever expect or believe that anyone can meet the "50 years to forever" expectation.

Fortunately or unfortunately, people other than our spouse do not suddenly become unattractive after we say, "I do." In fact, they generally become better looking as we settle into the everyday conundrum of matrimony. In spite of everything, this notion that marriages are destined to last forever, particularly monogamous marriages, appears unnatural. We must deny all of our innate emotional and physical inclinations and adopt a social value system as the natural order of human development. Herein we find a prime example of how we expect nurture to supersede nature.

Various sociological and anthropological studies indicate that 80% to 95% of all cultures in the world practice polygamy (having multiple partners) in one form or another.[10] That means that a mere 5% to 20% of the world's societies adhere to the monogamous marriage concept. It would be more practical to take a position that believes that this statistic indicates nature's influence on our societies. In other words, if 95% of the cultures in the world think that remaining committed to only one person over a lifetime is unrealistic, then they may be on to something. We can further conclude that the outstanding 5% may be off-center in their way of thinking.

I often wonder why Western cultures have developed the marriage is forever mentality. Firstly, to believe and expect a marriage to last forever is tremendously irrational in that no one lives forever. In this case, we anticipate the 50-year marriage myth to outlast our lifetime. We downgrade the forever expectation to a metaphor that many set as a tangible and an obtainable goal. Nevertheless, we find that our high marital expectations may set us up for a great degree of disappointment.

The metaphor of the forever marriage persists despite overwhelming evidence to the contrary. It is as though many potential couples believe they will jinx their marriage if they consider actual marriage and divorce statistics before they marry. Others interpret realistic analyses of actual marital outcomes by the proposed couple as unwarranted pessimism. They also feel that pondering the possibilities and causes of a failed marriage suggests that a supernatural, negative influence will unavoidably cause the same thing to happen to their relationships. Yet, most would agree that optimism offers no guarantee of matrimonial success or its stability. If hope were the missing element that offered security for a happy marriage, then there would be a minimal number of divorces in this country. This would be due in part to the fact that practically all marriages begin with the unbounded optimism of eternal marital bliss. Likewise, if we accept this, we could also conclude that pessimism has little or no affect on marital success or failure.

We, therefore, should think about exactly where the metaphor of the "forever marriage" originated. Some argue that our monogamous ideology is nature driven. This argument exists primarily because certain species of animals select and remain with only one sexual mate throughout their lifespan. However, as is with the case of Homo sapiens (humans), there are relatively few animals, when compared to the whole animal kingdom, that actually practice monogamy.[11] Most animals, including insects, follow the natural inclination to establish sexual relationships with several mates in an effort to guarantee the spread of their genes. Therefore, we can conclude that there is an inherent weakness in the argument for a natural drive to be monogamous.

Others believe that our one marriage, to one spouse, in one lifetime philosophy has monotheistic roots (belief in one God). From monotheism stems the notions of the "best," the "ideal," and the "only," as in the best college, the best job, the ideal marriage, the ideal wife, the only way, the only God, etc. This ultimate line of thinking leads to the streamlining of our social and lifelong goals. We then, analyze, interpret, and plot our personal histories along a linear continuum. We are born, we learn, we work, we marry, we bear children, we form a family, we retire, and we die (Figure 1).

LINEAR LIFELINE CONTINUUM

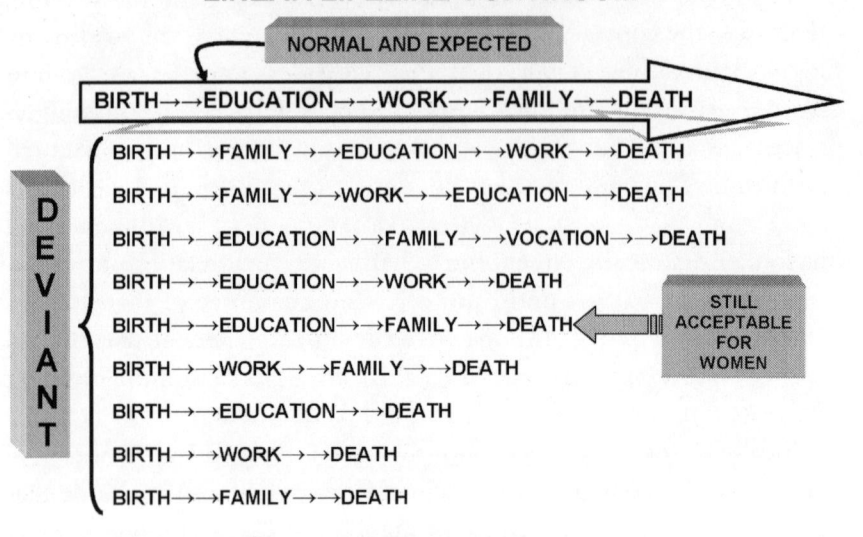

NORMAL AND EXPECTED

BIRTH→→EDUCATION→→WORK→→FAMILY→→DEATH

DEVIANT:
- BIRTH→→FAMILY→→EDUCATION→→WORK→→DEATH
- BIRTH→→FAMILY→→WORK→→EDUCATION→→DEATH
- BIRTH→→EDUCATION→→FAMILY→→VOCATION→→DEATH
- BIRTH→→EDUCATION→→WORK→→DEATH
- BIRTH→→EDUCATION→→FAMILY→→DEATH ← STILL ACCEPTABLE FOR WOMEN
- BIRTH→→WORK→→FAMILY→→DEATH
- BIRTH→→EDUCATION→→DEATH
- BIRTH→→WORK→→DEATH
- BIRTH→→FAMILY→→DEATH

FIGURE 1

Henceforth, our entire existence involves aspiring to attain the ideal-type position or level at every stage of our life. Society considers any type of deviation from the linear continuum to be an abnormal lifestyle (Figure 1). Consequently, many of us pursue this ultimate idealism without hesitation and never question its origin or validity. We simply do what we are socially programmed and, subsequently, expected to do. This is irrational—socially satisfying, but irrational, nonetheless.

On the other hand, some polytheists (those who worship more than one god) usually do not follow the mono-linear or unilateral idealistic model. Polytheists, as a practice, adopt the position that, simply put, more is better. In other words, individuals more greatly benefit, socially, by establishing relationships with several people. They respect and value several ideological perspectives. Therefore, they have not developed the "best," "only," or the "ideal" model of viewing the world. For polytheists, there is no concept of the best school because they feel students can glean knowledge from every school of thought. Thus, the more ideas and concepts they come to know, the more well rounded they become.

Additionally, polytheists have a respect for several gods because they believe that they can obtain broader spiritual awareness by establishing relationships with several celestial entities. They demonstrate this polytheistic foundation in their attitudes towards marriage also. In patriarchal, polygamous cultures, there is an underlying belief that having several female companions enhances a male's manhood. Subsequently, the more wives he has, the greater his status in the community.[12]

There may be some rational validity to the polygamous position in that there is a greater opportunity to learn invaluable social lessons from more than one individual. Assuredly, if a husband can keep the peace in a house full of women who have extremely varying personalities and dispositions, he may emerge in the end as a commendable people manager. The same holds true for women in matriarchal, polygamous societies.

The question then arises, why is remaining married to only one individual over a lifetime so important? Recent American social practices show a pattern of "serial monogamy."[13] Serial monogamy is the practice of dating or being married to only one person at a time, yet having several relationships over a lifetime. Studies also show that "approximately 75% of divorced people remarry…and some remarry, divorce, and remarry again (often referred to as serial divorce). Typically the length of time between divorce and remarriage is less than 4 years."[14] Clearly, there would be little or no need for our serial monogamous or serial divorcing behavior if our "only one companion, in one lifetime" mate selection process was successful or even reasonable. Still, the deeply rooted desire to find, connect with, and cling to that one special mate persists in many of us.

The 50-year to forever metaphor, often cements us into relationships that we probably should have dissolved many months or years prior. The hope of marital longevity overpowers our objective thinking. Unfortunately, idealistic and unsound optimism generates unclear, untested, and unsubstantiated edicts, old wives' tales, myths, metaphors, and expectations. This revelation came to me while I sat at a Caribbean Poker table in Costa Rica. When I sat down at the table, I felt what I am sure every poker player at the table felt—the gleeful hope and anticipation that each card the dealer overturned would bring me instant fortune. I found myself thinking that if only I did not count my poker chips then I would somehow get an advantage. In addition, I believed if I shuffled my cards before I looked at them, and I got a good hand to play, then thereafter I should always shuffle my cards before I turned them over. I began to develop even more superstitions as I continued to play. What was fascinating was that my superstitious behaviors carried on even though I stopped receiving favorable hands. Still, the powerful hope of success in the next deck of cards kept my expectations alive.

I compare this same emotional and behavioral dynamic to our attitudes towards marriage. Many of us have deep-seeded expectations that our marriages will endure no matter what obstacles we encounter throughout the relationship. This cheerful anticipation of marital permanence produces a strong desire to find and identify the secret formula for matrimonial success. Since no clear formula actually exists, we tend to grasp hold to the edicts, superstitions, metaphors, and old wives tales passed down to us by our family and other social institutions like, school, church, and the media. For example, age-old myths like, "love conquers all," "love heals all wounds," "If you love them and they are meant for you then let them go and they will always return," "true love lasts forever," "marriage was meant to last," "true love never cheats," etc. We, subsequently, incorporate these ideas into our mate selection practices even though they show no proof whatsoever that they have any affect on the outcome of our relationships. In actuality, these same metaphors may indeed spawn unrealistic and unattainable expectations. These unfulfilled expectations are commonly what lead to conflicts in a marriage.

Further, marriage remains one of the only contracts recognized between willing participants that we suppose to last for a lifetime. The courts even support the long-lasting durability of this social institution. Whether a couple has been married 5 years or 50 years, if they want to dissolve the marriage, they will have to wade through a swamp of legal formalities. In contrast, automobile purchase agreements generally last for only four or five years. Even real estate purchases have only a 30 or 40-year commitment—and you can usually pay off the mortgages early with little or no legal repercussion. Further, you can change your mind midway through the commitment period and upgrade your appliance, automobile, or home purchase while getting sincere praise from your family, friends, and neighbors. This is not so with the marriage contract, however. Try telling everyone halfway through your marriage that you have changed your mind and decided to upgrade, or that you want to opt out of your contract. Now sit back and watch the social sanctions fly.

It is as if once you have decided to enter into a marriage, you willingly and irrevocably sell yourself over as an indentured servant. Furthermore, you have given up your right to change your mind and opt out of the deal without consequence. Unlike professional athletes who continuously renegotiate their contract based on past and present performance, no matter how well or poorly we perform in our marriage, we are still locked into our 50- year to forever pledge.

Again, I present the question of why is there such a necessity to accomplish lifelong monogamy. Moreover, why is this need so overpowering? After rational analysis, we can conclude that establishing several monogamous relationships over a lifetime may be more beneficial to all parties. It may be that the 50-year to forever expectation breeds the dread of being locked into an unfulfilling marriage. This internalized anxiety, subsequently, may induce unwarranted tension and stress upon the relationship causing one or both individuals to decide eventually to end the marriage.

By abolishing the expectation of longstanding marriages, we leave spouses the invaluable hope of escape without the threat of negative social sanctioning. This action, thereby, may lesson the fear and the consequential strain present in many marriages. Arresting the hope of a lifelong marital commitment, oddly enough, may lead to longer marriages as couples stay together because they want to and not because they have to out of the fear of sacrificing social acceptance.

Marriage and the NIKE™ Approach: *"Just Do It"*

"What luck of rulers that men do not think."
Adolf Hitler

Often my conscience gets the best of me and I feel somewhat guilty for, what many say, attacking the current ideas about love and marriage. Many times when I discuss these controversial concepts in class with my students or with my colleagues and friends, they tend to make me out to be the bad guy. They commonly pose me as the villain because I question the core values and beliefs that often form the foundation of our existence. I too wonder sometimes of the fairness of pulling the proverbial rug of social comfort from beneath the feet of those I speak to about love and marriage. Then I remind myself that I am a sociology professor and that is why they pay me—that always seems to make me feel a little better. Nevertheless, the vilification of me, and those who have similar ideas that question the normal behavior of groups, persists.

It is as though the very existence of a traditional ritual or way of thinking legitimizes and cements it into place. Subsequently, many view anyone who goes against the social grain with suspicion. I, on the other hand, believe that all ideologies are and should be open to question and, yes, scrutiny. This idea checking may keep the moral entrepreneurs[15] like the Heartbrokers,[16] Marriagebrokers, Religiousbrokers, and the

Politicalbrokers from committing abominable acts against society. Historians have over the years recorded examples of such acts—the Inquisition Period, for example. During that period, the governing elite and the preservers of church doctrine severely punished anyone who presented a way of thinking that was contrary to theirs. The content of the dissenting ideas was not important. What was important, however, was that the dissenters did not go against the pre-established social order of things. Consequently, under the fear and threat of public ridicule, imprisonment, and possible death people simply lived and thought as expected. It was only at the introduction of the Enlightenment Period (1600-1700's)[17] that people began to embrace other channels of thought and rational ideology. Acceptance of these new or merely different ways of thinking did not come easily, however. Nevertheless, society over time far less vilified free thinkers. Society eventually gave credibility to philosophers and theorists of all sorts.

Today, although the threat of severe punitive reprisal by the governing elite is almost nonexistent, members of almost every society still rarely go against the social grain. We generally take for granted that the way things are are the way things are supposed to be. We do not question these social processes. We do not exam them. We do not contest them. We plainly embrace them as the natural order of life. As a result, we adopt the NIKE™ approach to our entire social existence—we "just do it." Unfortunately, society punishes, in one way or another, those of us who are not as willing to "just do it" like everyone else.

In hindsight, I can see the relevance of the NIKE™ mentality towards marriage and other intimate relationships. It was considerably simpler for me to go along with the natural flow of my emotional and social programming. I was free of the responsibility of making a logical analysis of my life's decisions. Everyone within my social circles figuratively and literally applauded my actions. Consequently, my life mirrored the lives of my neighbors, friends, colleagues, and general acquaintances. It was so much easier back then.

Fortunately or unfortunately—depending on how you interpret it—I took on the burden of actually thinking about and even questioning the everyday choices and actions that I undertook. I, consequently, developed the courage or madness—again it depends on how you look at it—to step outside of the confines of convention. I began to challenge individual interpretations of right and wrong. I did not "just do it" anymore. I "just questioned it." It was at this juncture where life ceased to be easy for me. Rational thinking forced me from my comfort zone. Before, I always chose the path of life that posed the least resistance. The choice was easy in that social stigma and dissatisfaction accompanied the alternatives.

Regrettably, the function of the NIKE™ mentality only serves to distract us from the realities of everyday life. Particularly, it sidetracks us from the actuality of the marital institution. Hope supersedes logic. Optimism circumvents common sense. However, we should not leave the institution of marriage to chance if we still expect it to be a lifelong venture.

We must not confuse cautious and rational analysis with unnecessary pessimism. Many of us have more regard for the various investments we make that we do not expect to yield as great of a reward as our marriages. We spend countless hours researching possible commitments and investments before we make up our minds. We even consult with experts in the field where we plan to explore. We hire consultants and study vast amounts of literature. Consequently, when we make our investment decision, it is usually from an enlightened position. The "just do it" approach to financial investments and career decisions seem reckless, ludicrous, and fool-hearty. How much more ridiculous does the "just do it" mindset sound when we apply it to our lifelong marital investments?

Instead of slapping the wrists of those who point out the inherent pitfalls of marriage, we should give them the same respect and validity that we give to our stockbrokers, college counselors, employers, or our computer technicians. Today's so-called marriagebrokers are the only ones who seem to have attained this position of knowledge and expertise. The way we qualify them, however, is extremely bothersome to me. I am troubled primarily because the marriagebrokers consistently circulate the NIKE™ attitude towards love and marriage without restriction. "Just do it and God will take care of the rest...," they say. "Just do it and love will find a way," they proclaim. "Just do it and let life take its course." What if you walked into an investment firm and consulted a stockbroker on how, when, where, and why you should invest your money with them? What if he told you, "Ahh, don't worry about a thing, just do it and let the stock market take its course"? Would you plop down your hard-earned cash on his desk, shake his hand, thank him for his invaluable advice and leave?

What if you went to your school counselor for academic advice on choosing relevant courses for your intended career? What if she simply handed you the school catalogue and told you to close your eyes and point to a course, any course? What if after you questioned her counseling techniques she told you to, "relax and just do it, the educational system will find a way"? How about if your computer crashed and you needed to call a technician? What if, after you explained to her what happened, she pleasantly told you with the utmost confidence to switch on the power and let technology take care of the rest? No instructions, no diagrams or blueprints…Just do it!!!

Clearly, the NIKE™ approach does not work in these instances and neither will it work when it comes to choosing what you hope to be your lifelong companion. We should adopt a "just think about it first" mindset as a substitute for the "just do it" attitude. Moreover, we should practice a "just let me do a little research or read a few books and articles on the subject first" approach before we get married.

Entering into a relationship with blind, reckless ambition fueled only by unfounded marital guidelines and expectations will eventually have the same outcome as entering into any investment venture ignorantly and without proper preparation. Some people who blindly play the stock market get lucky and obtain untold fortune. However, way more often then not, less than well-informed investors end up squandering their life's savings on a whim and a dream. Those who consult ill-informed marriagebrokers fare no better in their relationships.

Many of us spend years in school preparing for our careers. Yet, we spend only a few minutes, maybe a few hours preparing for our marriages. It is no wonder why the divorce rate in this country is over 50%. Unlike many professions where we can learn on the job, marriage does not afford us the same luxury. This is primarily due to the fact that by the time we receive adequate experience in matrimony, many of the breeches that occur in our relationships are far beyond repair—and all of the training in the world cannot prepare us to work out a problem-riddled marriage.

Marriage and Religion: *The Religious Marriagebrokers*

"When a prophet speaketh in the name of the Lord, if the thing follow not, nor come to pass, that is the thing which the Lord hath not spoken."
Anonymous

The individuals in practically every culture that seem to sustain the most influence on marital ideas and practices are the religious leaders. I often refer to them as religious marriagebrokers. These self-appointed marital experts include local pastors, priests, tele-evangelists, and other clergy. Most religious marriagebrokers have little or no formal education or training on the subject of marriage, however. Yet, they do have a wealth of information that they eagerly share with prospective brides and grooms.

Spiritual marriagebrokers generally use the Bible, Torah, Koran, or other sacred catechisms as foundations for their philosophies about marriage. The religious marriagebrokers' sacred calling authenticates their expertise in all aspects of social life—including marriage. Further, history shows that in many cultures a direct link exists between one's spiritual relationship with God, the gods, or other supreme beings and their attitude towards marriage. This link empowers the church and its representatives as the absolute marriagebrokers in many societies, even today.

Ultimate empowerment, however, proves challenging when we try to establish workable marriages, primarily, because of the *spiritualization* of matrimony. The process of spiritualization does not leave room for the rational application of practical premarital ideas. For example, spiritual marriagebrokers encourage would-be brides and grooms to seek supernatural consultation from God or the gods when they confront marital questions or problems and when selecting a mate. However, the spiritual application of divine concepts to non-spiritual relationships is extremely irrational. Religious marriagebrokers commonly encourage religious believers to retreat to a private place and pray when issues in their marriage arise. Believers, therefore, pray hoping that a higher source will intercede on their behalf, thus fixing the problem. However, this optimism of spiritual intervention relieves the believer of the responsibility of rationally evaluating the exact source of marital conflict. Moreover, if the conflict is resolved soon after a believer seeks divine intercession, the religious marriagebrokers get the credit. On the other hand, if after they send up prayers and no positive changes occur in the marriage, the religious marriagebrokers accuse the believer of improperly applying their marital success guidelines. Additionally, they simply charge off the unsuccessful marriages to one or more of the believers being out of favor with God or the gods. Consequently, the spiritual marriagebrokers maintain their legitimate place as the expert relationship advisers.

Unfortunately, the absence of logical analysis leaves behind no tangible evidence of what exactly leads to marital success. This is primarily because miraculous intercessions by supreme sources do not require or obligate them to reveal their formula for success. Faith, then, is the only prerequisite for marital satisfaction. Hence, we find, according to the religious marriagebrokers, that the primary ingredient for a spiritually, socially, personally, and physically satisfying marriage is not thinking or acting, but believing. Faith, however, is subjective and open to argument. Substantial, rational, or physical proof of the achievements or value of the religious marriagebrokers' philosophies is never necessary. In fact, the more a believer questions their marital statutes and concepts the more the religious marriagebrokers charge them with the doubting of and being disloyal to the sacred doctrine. Consequently, most religious members find emotional and spiritual contentment in blindly following the religious marriagebrokers' matrimonial principles.

This forms the basis of my skepticism of the validity of the religious marriagebrokers' place in society. For example, it is difficult to use the Bible as the keystone of the marriage ideology. This is, principally, because there are no clear and comprehensive examples of successful marriages anywhere in the scriptures. Neither the Old nor the New Testament boasts of individuals who could serve as the perfect marriage models for believers to mimic (Table 1). For example, Adam was doing just fine until Eve came along. Abraham slept with his handmaid, Hagar.[18] Jacob had two wives. He loved one, Rachel, and hated the other, Leah.[19] David had one of his own officers killed so he could be with his wife.[20] The only two women Samson cared about tricked and ultimately betrayed him.[21] Moses abandoned his wife and family to do the work of God.[22] Solomon had seven hundred wives and three hundred concubines.[23] Most of the Old Testament prophets were not married; no documents appear to exist for those who were. The disciples of the New Testament also abandoned their wives and families to follow Jesus. The Apostle Paul encouraged the church members not to marry but to remain single like him.[24] Even Jesus Christ himself was not married.

Biblical Characters and Marital Relationships

Character	Attitude Towards Marriage
Abraham	Slept with his handmaid to conceive a child
Jacob	Had two wives, hated one, Leah, and loved the other, Rachel
Moses	Abandoned his wife and family to do the work of God
Samson	Betrayed by the only two women he cared about
Solomon	Had 700 wives and 300 concubines
Job	His wife abandoned him in his time of need
David	Killed the husband of the woman he wanted for himself
Jesus	He was single
Paul	He was single
Disciples	Abandoned their families to follow Jesus

Table 1

Clearly, there is no pattern or formula for marital bliss outlined in the Bible. Additionally, there are scarce and scattered references to marriage throughout. Jesus Christ seemed annoyed when the Sadducees [25] questioned him about marital policies and issues.[26] It is difficult to find instances in the Bible where Jesus and the other prophets found the topic of marriage so important as to address it extensively. Still, the authenticity of the religious marriagebrokers' unfounded principles continue unchallenged.

Someone recently emailed me a note entitled, "Jesus knows how to treat a woman." The email outlined several areas where Jesus supplied both the emotional and spiritual needs of a woman. It ended with the phrase, "So if you want to know how to treat your wife, do as Jesus does." I thought this was a cute little message, so I wrote her back and said, "I see your point, but Jesus was still smart enough not to get married."

The question arises, how then are the religious marriagebrokers still able to, so confidently, claim the marriage mastery? Their marriages also experience problems and breakdowns. Notwithstanding, we go on idolizing their less than conventional matrimonial notions. Further, the proficiency of their influence penetrates well within the family structure. Religious marriagebrokers are instrumental in establishing family role expectations. Women are frequently encouraged to be subject to the will and wishes of their husbands. Additionally, many religions expect husbands to take the leadership role in the household. The marital hierarchy involves putting God first in all things. Secondly, the requirements of and obligations to the church are equally essential and must be met. The needs of the family rank third in the hierarchy. Finally, individual interests and aspirations place last on the matrimonial continuum.

The wives generally sacrifice their personal happiness and take pride in the servitude aspect of the marriage—so it would appear. According to the religious marriagebrokers, the path to ultimate happiness for the wife lies in complete self-denial. Nevertheless, after critical analysis, their position looks questionable in practical application in that they believe the path to happiness rests in depriving themselves of the very things that make them happy.

Likewise, the religious marriagebrokers suggest that husbands devalue striving to attain their personal goals in the face of their obligations to his God, his church, and his family. Henceforth, he achieves marital bliss, paradoxically, by channeling his happiness through others first. He eventually internalizes that there is little or no pleasure that is equivalent to this new community based contentment.

Unfortunately, this ideological foundation weakens when everyday marital interactions breed confusion and conflict. Notwithstanding, in these instances, faith and hope remain the lone avenues of emotional escape for the husband and the wife. Nevertheless, even with faith and hope at their disposal, marital discontentment persists within the confines of religiously based families. As a result, divorces are still prevalent among religious believers.

Despite the lack of clear-cut evidence that their marriage success policies are effective, the religious marriagebrokers continue to spread ambiguous remedies for an ever-growing problem. Logical thinking and faith are usually not compatible. Individuals must make a choice. Logical thinking in relation to spiritual doctrine is discouraged and deemed as signs of rebellion against God, the gods, or their representatives. Nevertheless, if religiously motivated couples desire to salvage their marriages, it is imperative that they rebel to some degree against the misguided and ill-founded marriage rules established by the religious marriagebrokers.

When religious marriagebrokers critically evaluate other more balanced viewpoints they conclude that the logical stances are irreverent, Godless, and self-serving. Members of some religious arenas actively shun and avoid each of these attributes. Conversely, if rational observers examine the religious marriagebrokers' nuptial ideologies they will determine that the religious concepts and solutions to common marriage issues are, at best, mythical and illogical.

The mainstays of the religious marriagebrokers involve the notions of faith, hope, submission, and patience. Each of these notable aspects of the religious marriage offers a temporary emotional and psychological escape from the problems at hand. However, none requires proactive, solid, or measurable action. They suppose that if believers live according to the belief system outlined in the Bible or other sacred sources, God or the gods will reveal to them the prescription for a fulfilling marriage.

The intercessor, in theory, will stimulate a miraculous change in their attitude towards marriage. This enables the believer to further submit to the marriage institution and accept the burdensome problems as a natural trying of their faith. In other words, the constant marital conflicts are tools utilized by a higher source to strengthen them spiritually. As a result, the more the believer is willing and able to endure the longsuffering of marriage the closer he comes to his God or the gods. This may explain why even after thousands of years there does not exist a tried and true formula for relationship harmony in religious culture. Identifying the recipe for marital bliss is not as important to the believer as the spiritual strength she gains by enduring a problem-filled marriage.

The Bible does talk about the inbuilt difficulties present in most marriages. For example, it states that, "They that marry shall have trouble in the flesh."[27] This particular scripture attests to the inescapable consequences that occur when two people from two distinctive social circles choose to inhabit the same household on an intimate level. Although the Bible warns believers of the impending hardships of matrimony, it falls short of explaining how to alleviate or avoid these problems. Believers are left to apply the intangible principles—again, faith, hope, submission, and patience—to tangible and logical problematic marital situations. In other words, is it possible to pray, believe, or hope away sexually related issues in a marriage? Further, should anyone realistically, patiently endure and remain submissive in the face of the unalterable personality conflicts and ideological differences? Moreover, should they tolerate physical and or emotional abuse and have faith that deliverance will come eventually?

One reference in the Bible addresses a possible practical solution for troubles that may arise in the home between a husband and wife. The book of Proverbs states, "It is better to dwell upon a rooftop than in a house with an odious and contentious woman."[28] We can interpret this type of remedy as escapism. I actually knew someone—a preacher—who tried this solution. One time when his wife worked his nerves to a point where he could no longer bear it, he went into the garage and got a ladder. He proceeded to climb up on the roof of his house. Once on top, he kicked the ladder down. After a few hours and as darkness began to fall, he called out to his wife to retrieve the ladder so he could climb down. When he finally climbed down from the rooftop, he still had to confront the issues that drove him up the ladder in the first place. This is a prime example of how even biblically based solutions to marital conflicts become ineffective through practical application.

Submission is another vital feature of the religious marital ideology. This premise also seems to sidestep the responsibility of critically analyzing the matter-of-fact nature of marriage. For this reason, believers simply retreat and submit when problems arise. Understand that there is nothing wrong, per se, with this strategy. A couple will definitely dodge confrontations in their marriage if they practice this approach—particularly if both parties simultaneously submit to each other. Notwithstanding, anyone who follows the path of submissiveness will find that, in the long run, their marital problems still persist as they continue to go unaddressed. They only change their attitude towards the problem—which may not be a bad remedy.

Some believers may experience spiritual satisfaction while performing their compliant acts. However, the resentment they harbor when they continually surrender to the whims and wishes of their spouse may trigger secondary psychological concerns. For example, most religions usually expect women to be submissive to their husbands. Subsequently, the social role expectations of the wife become the source of marital happiness and spiritual salvation for her. She, then, fulfills her wifely duties, not because she wants to, but because she has to in order to obtain and retain social acceptance. After awhile, her personal identity and desire for contentment intertwine with her societal and sacred obligations. Hence, we find that she does not actually choose her avenues of pleasure. Her personal satisfaction rests with the fulfillment of everyone else's expectations. Over time, she may rebel. However, her rebellion remains within socially accepted guidelines. For instance, she may completely immerse herself in the service-oriented roles associated with marriage. Many submissive wives begin to downgrade sexual intimacy with their husband to a social and spiritual obligation rather than a personal and pleasurable experience. Her actions, in turn, deprive her husband of intimate relations with his wife. Consequently, she forces her husband to make a choice. He must either encourage her to pursue personal pleasure and contentment, thus, possibly generating an increase in intimate interaction. He does this knowing that his wife's pursuit of happiness may lead to a decline in meeting her religious and social obligations. Alternatively, he can continue to insist that she carry out her predetermined marital duties and accept the decline in intimacy in the name of religion. The wife often unconsciously and sometimes consciously initiates this act of passive aggression. As a result, the deterioration of sexual closeness remains a chief motivator for divorce even in the church.

Clearly, although a religious couple stays married, it does not mean that their union is successful or ideal. They may continue with the marriage simply going through the motions in order to execute their dutiful responsibilities. Rational marital analysis involves taking into consideration the actual elements that may lead to marital conflict and happiness. It also offers couples the flexibility of choice, which allows them an avenue of escape in the event of a hopeless marriage. Contrary to the expectations of the religious marriagebrokers, longsuffering and patience are not acceptable alternatives when the logical choice is to abandon an extremely bad marriage arrangement. Rationalism leaves little room for faith, hope, submission, and patience when attempting to resolve problems in a marriage. There is only room for logical action. Although the choices may not be popular from a social standpoint, they may indeed be necessary for a couple's emotional and even spiritual health.

Marriage and Expectations: *At Your Service*

"If divorce has increased by one thousand percent, don't blame the women's movement. Blame the obsolete sex roles on which our marriages were based."
Betty Friedan

The marriagebrokers have laid out a roadmap for us to follow once we decide to get married. They have written the marriage script and all we have to do is play out the roles. These roles are distinct for both the husband and the wife. Whenever we marry, we, basically, meld into our predetermined marital trade without question. However, if you have not figured it out by now, my major objective for writing this book is to provoke you to, at the very least, think about and question the hows and whys of your daily decisions and behaviors, especially concerning marriage. The more I begin to think about my relationships, as opposed to just performing certain tasks, the more I become aware of the pointlessness of these pre-established roles and expectations. It is as though our individuality is lost to these predetermined social guidelines. The roles, therefore, have become significantly more essential than the role-players have. Moreover, the character requirements also become more valuable than us. However, if marriages are to endure and progress satisfactorily, the role-players must have equal importance. To illustrate, in film and in stage plays many low-talent actors have spoiled countless roles. Their less than stellar performances negatively affect the entire production. It is not that a lot of work did not go into developing the role, but the producers placed too little emphasis on refining the role-player. Marriages are no different when it comes to giving special attention to the actors. We expect husbands and wives to execute their preset marriage roles without placing much weight on their personal happiness. Furthermore, they do not perform their roles out of free choice. On the contrary, they perform their tasks out of communal obligation. Society has programmed us to believe that our source of personal contentment is rooted in the accomplishment of these social requirements. As a result, both men and women tend to gauge their value as a man or woman purely on the amount of service-oriented tasks they perform for members of their families. In other words, the more a man caters to and provides for his family, the more manly he feels. Concurrently, the more manly he feels the happier he believes he is. Therefore, he finds happiness in the outward acts of servitude and that his satisfaction is not inwardly motivated. Of course, the same goes for women (Figure 2).

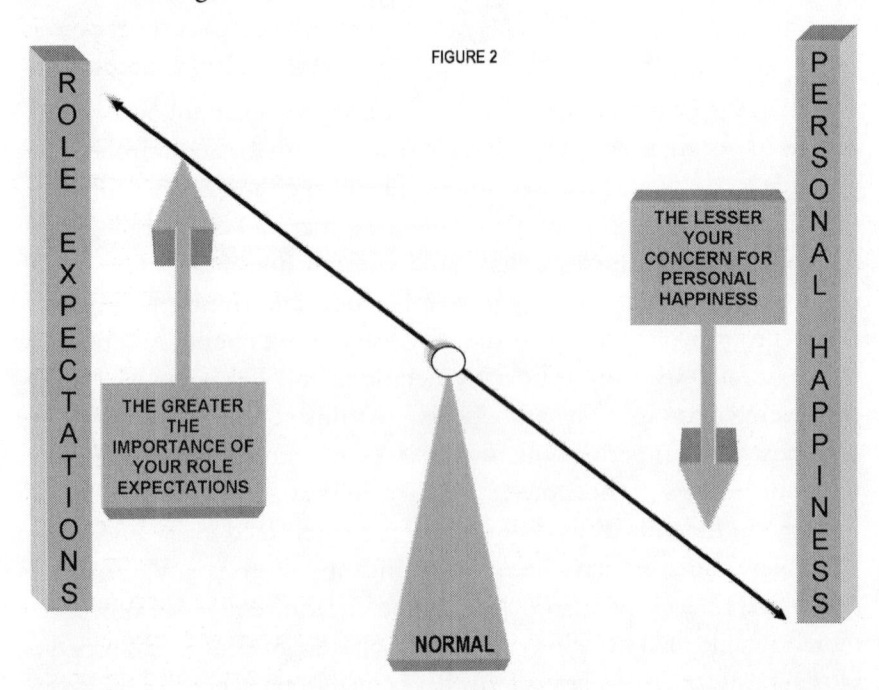

FIGURE 2

THE GREATER THE IMPORTANCE OF YOUR ROLE EXPECTATIONS

THE LESSER YOUR CONCERN FOR PERSONAL HAPPINESS

ROLE EXPECTATIONS

PERSONAL HAPPINESS

NORMAL

We are constantly expected to prove our love for our significant others through outward expression. We do this by enthusiastically carrying out our marital tasks. Stereotypically, a wife shows her love for her husband by cooking and cleaning for him and taking care of his children. A husband, in turn, proves his regard for his wife by providing for her and offering her protection and emotional support. We find that, in a traditional marriage love without works is empty.

After rational evaluation of the institution of marriage, it is clear that our prime motivation to marry stems from the expectation that our spouse will perform certain and distinct duties in the marriage. If they do not meet their mutual obligations, we often dissolve the marriage. Again, we find then that these social role obligations are more essential than the spouse is. Clearly, there is nothing wrong with expecting your husband or wife to perform certain duties around the home. Historically, the distribution of household chores was the central reason why people decided to marry in the first place.[29] In the past, people usually married someone who was able to undertake the tasks that they did not have the time or the skill to complete. However, today individuals are inclined to believe that the prime motivation to wed is love. They, therefore, unknowingly generate unrealistic expectations in their marriages.

Many of us would avoid experiencing unnecessary problems if we would let our prospective mates know the particulars of our marital role requirements before the wedding. If, at the beginning, we would highlight exactly what we expect our spouse to do and focus less on cultivating our romantic love expectations we would conceivably have a clearer picture of the future health of our marriage.

Because of the evolution or devolution of the gender roles in society today, whereas men and women are starting to share familial duties, spouses should not assume the traditional role requirements. Husbands are not automatically automobile mechanics, gardeners, plumbers, carpenters, butlers, repairmen, or chauffeurs simply because they are males who got married. Additionally, wives are not naturally house cleaners, cooks, dishwashers, babysitters, grocery stockers, accountants, or caretakers because they happen to be women who got married.

These gender role requirements are rooted in old-fashioned ideologies that have little relevance in today's evolving marital perspectives.

Many couples want to establish a contemporary relationship based on traditional beliefs. This mindset may be irrational and, subsequently, challenging. A mixing of the old and the new can cause other issues. For example, today there is far less of a stigma associated with a woman who chooses to work outside of the home. Consequently, there are more women in the workforce than ever before. Yet, society still expects women to perform the majority of the domestic chores around the home. These chores usually center on cooking, cleaning, and taking care of the children. This dual role expectation may create problems in the area of intimacy between spouses. Problems occur primarily because she spends considerable time working outside of the home and fulfilling her domestic responsibilities. She, therefore, has little time or energy left to cultivate an intimate relationship with her husband.

Again, it is clear that personal and even matrimonial happiness takes a back seat to accomplishing our family goals—and many of us see nothing wrong with that. However, the same people seem to ignore the connection between the lack of individual contentment and the relatively high divorce rate in this country.

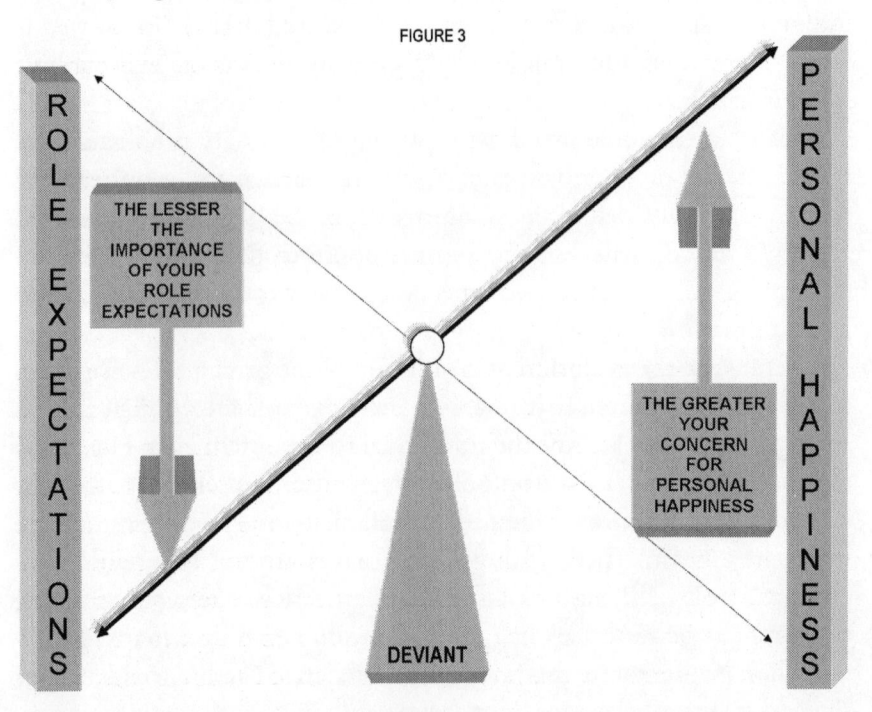

FIGURE 3

ROLE EXPECTATIONS

THE LESSER THE IMPORTANCE OF YOUR ROLE EXPECTATIONS

THE GREATER YOUR CONCERN FOR PERSONAL HAPPINESS

PERSONAL HAPPINESS

DEVIANT

Marriagebrokers

People generally ground their contemporary marriages in their personal fulfillment and their subsequent strong sense of freedom and independence. Traditional marriages deemphasize both. Henceforth, the more concerned spouses are with their individual happiness, the less they are worried about meeting their marital role expectations (Figure 3). Clearly, it is essential to a fresh marriage that a couple decide on what is more vital to them in advance. Neither the contemporary nor the traditional type of marriage arrangement is in itself good or bad. Furthermore, there is no proof that either is the best formula for marriage success and longevity. Notwithstanding, assuming that your spouse knows what you expect, in regard to your marital role expectations, is a tried and true prescription for matrimonial failure.

Once more, we must understand that our preordained gender roles are not as important as the marriage. Many couples marry to have someone satisfy the tasks that their parents previously performed. Recently, one of my students stated that she would only consider marrying a man who takes care of her like her father does. Obviously, her parent's expectant marital model supersedes the desires and maybe even the abilities of the prospective husband in this case.

Other couples envy and strive to imitate the lives of their parents. The lifestyles of their parents and grandparents seem to serve as successful models for satisfying the gender role expectations in the home. However, when they interview their parents and inquire about the degree of happiness they experience in their marriage, many express regret and discontentment. The basis of their unhappiness is rooted in the fact that many parents, for years, sacrifice their personal freedom and gratification for their pre-established marital and social responsibilities. One of my students shared with me that her mother, who has been married to her father for 18 years, read my book, *Heartbrokers*. She told me that after reading my book, her mother stated that she had wasted 18 years of her life trying to make everyone happy but herself. Her mother, subsequently, has set out to make up for all her lost time by finally indulging in the things she likes. Something she should have done years earlier. Situations like this may explain why many married couples experience the empty nest syndrome when their children finally leave home. It may be that they eventually realize that for the term of the union, their spouse and their marriage was always secondary to what everyone expected of them.

There is a paradigm or model of life and of living that may surpass the traditional idea of the family in its effectiveness. We may find pure contentment after we critically consider these alternate lifestyles. It is okay for each individual to define their marital roles and not let those pre-established guidelines define them.

Marriage and Power: *Heads or Tails?*

"Power creates its own resistance."
James Reston

There appears to be inconsistencies in relation to the distribution of power between a husband and wife. Today, women anticipate having as much say-so in marital affairs as their husbands. Matrimonial equity is not only implied but is also expected. However, the contradiction occurs when women, usually under the guise of romance and chivalry, look forward to different treatment. Many women feel that it sets them apart from all others when a man romances them and treat them like a lady. These romantic and chivalrous gestures usually include opening a door, pulling out a chair, helping with a coat, paying for a meal, offering economic support, supplying protection, etc. Some women not only expect men to do these tasks for them, but require them of their love interest. Clearly, there is nothing wrong with these acts of kindness in and of themselves. Strangers perform courteous deeds for each other on the streets everyday. However, these demonstrations of kindness, under the cloak of chivalry, only tend to reinforce the hierarchal differences between men and women.

Women, on the one hand, want equal and fair treatment. Yet, on the other hand, they demand special consideration. Unbeknownst to most women, however, this special treatment labels them as the weaker character in the relationship. Women often take pride and refuge in the quality of powerlessness. It is as if they crave, portray, and adorn themselves with frailty. Thus, for them feminine helplessness more readily identifies them as a lady. This frame of mind, nevertheless, could prove challenging for those who seek an equal distribution of power in a marriage (Figure 4). We find that the more chivalrous a man is towards his wife, the less equality exists in the relationship.

The concept of power between two or more individuals naturally denotes the existence of a stronger and a weaker unit. Without this differentiation, power would not exist. Women, therefore, who insist on unique handling, as the weaker person, should not and cannot expect to share equal power in their relationships—that would be irrational.

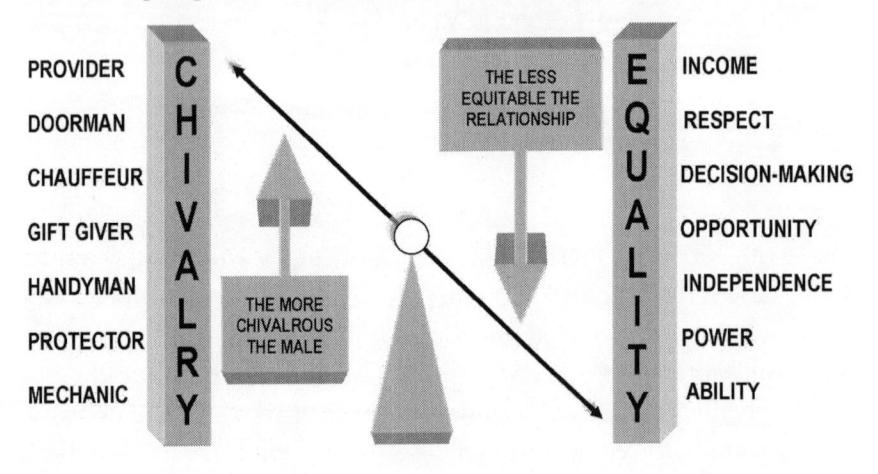

CHIVALRY		EQUALITY
PROVIDER	THE LESS EQUITABLE THE RELATIONSHIP	INCOME
DOORMAN		RESPECT
CHAUFFEUR		DECISION-MAKING
GIFT GIVER		OPPORTUNITY
HANDYMAN	THE MORE CHIVALROUS THE MALE	INDEPENDENCE
PROTECTOR		POWER
MECHANIC		ABILITY

FIGURE 4

It is not difficult to see why the idea of chivalry has continued to flourish in our society, however. Both the male and the female benefit tremendously, they feel, from these gallant acts. Women, many times, are on the receiving end of several male service-oriented tasks. They benefit because they often reap economic rewards as men regularly provide for them. As long as a man believes that it is his duty to pay for a woman's food, lodging, and her various pleasures, she does not have to expend her assets. She has a committed servant who is willing to open up her doors and aid her with other trivial tasks that she could otherwise do herself with little effort. Hence, females often reinforce the chivalrous male's behavior through positive sanctions like simple smiles, offering up kisses, giving him sex, taking care of his children, completing his domestic chores, etc. Undoubtedly, there is little motivation for women to suspend or discourage chivalry and romance.

Similarly, men also profit from their noble deeds. By consistently coming to the rescue of damsels in distress, men fortify within their psyche the importance of male dominance. Men sometimes force their chivalrous ways onto women—although most of the time, force is not necessary. The male bolsters his ego after each romantic act. Indeed, most of his personal satisfaction comes when others observe his gallant performances. Men often define their degree of manliness by these displays of chivalry. "A real man knows how to treat a lady," they say. Repeatedly, the more men do for women, the more they feel like men. Consequently, like women, our culture does not motivate chivalrous men to discontinue acts of gallantry because it is within some performances men find a sense of worth, their identity, and their source of power (Table 2).

Women, it seems, are their own worse enemy when it comes to the inequitable allocation of power in their intimate relationships. I cannot count the number of times I have heard women make circular statements like, "…let the man be the man…" or "I want a real gentleman…" They also underline the notion that wives should be submissive to their husbands. Subsequently, women, too, have come to define maleness in terms of what men do for them.

The more a man caters to a woman's supposed weakness, the more of a man he appears. "Real men do this…real men do that…" However, we can easily argue that acts of servitude do not substantiate a man's maleness or a woman's femaleness. The type of genitalia determines a male and female. A man is a man because he has a penis and testicles. Women are women because they have a vagina. A man is still a man even if he never opens a door for a woman. He is a man whether he pays for her meals and lodging. A man is a man even if he fails to help with a woman's coat or pulls out her chair. Men are men because they are born boys who become men not because society programs them to be romanticized slaves. Likewise, a woman is still a woman whether she cooks a meal, cleans a house, bears a child, changes a diaper, or washes a dish. She too is a woman because she was born a girl who grew into such and not because she is the glorified "Angel of the House."[30] Our servitude to our families should not form the foundation of our ideas and definitions of manliness and womanliness. Furthermore, they should not influence the way we allocate power in a marriage.

Effects of Chivalry

	Men	Women
Inequitable Romantic Relationships	Reinforces dominance Feels more manly Willing romantic servant	Reinforces inequality Feels special Needs provided for
Equitable Less Romantic Relationships	Reinforces equality Feels less manly Less romantic	Reinforces equality Feels less special Satisfies own needs

Table 2

Noted author, Stephanie Coontz, in her book, *The Way We Never Were*,[31] asserts that, when viewed historically, marriage and inequitable power distribution between males and females was far from reality. In the early 1600's the family construct and the distribution of power was far more equitable. According to Coontz, both the husband and the wife were responsible for providing for and the protection, education, and nurturing of the family. Chivalry gave way to necessity, as survival was exceedingly more important than romance or power. By the late 1700's a dichotomization or splitting of familial roles took place in our society. Events like the Revolutionary War, the onset of capitalism, and the Industrial Revolution prompted these changes. Women, subsequently, began to trade their equal status and control in the family for economic support and protection. In turn, men had their domestic needs met. This division of labor within the family eventually evolved into an unequal distribution of power between men and women in the home.

Additionally, Coontz asserts that society reserved the personality traits associated with being the educator and the nurturer in the family (kindness, sensitivity, caring, submissive, understanding, and emotional) for the wife. Conversely, men adopted the attributes related to the provider and protector (strength, courage, dedication, aggression, logic, and insensitivity). This separation and distinguishing of personality traits, as well as familial responsibility, was in direct contrast to the time when both men and women performed the same functions in the household and, subsequently, had similar personality characteristics.

Today, one of the worst insults to a man is to associate him with the stereotypical personality attributes reserved for women. The same holds true for women in respect to associating them with masculine tendencies. The social authorities exploit and commercialize these stereotypical gender-based qualities and utilize them to cement members of society into their place in the hierarchy of power.

The religious marriagebrokers contend that ultimate power in a marriage is a god-given right set aside expressly for men. Women, then, should not only honor God or the gods, but the marriagebrokers also expect them to respect and reverence their husbands. Moreover, religion justifies the supposed power husbands exert over his wife. This is, essentially, because we commonly think of God in terms of being a male. The interpretation of God as a man is not surprising in that those who wrote and canonized the bible were predominantly male. Yet, the Bible, in many instances, refutes the significance of gender. For example, Jesus told the Sadducees and the Pharisees (the religious experts of the day) that there is neither male nor female in heaven.[32] Since God is a spirit and a spirit has no physical characteristics that distinguish it as male or female, how can we conclude that God is a male? Clearly, the prejudices and restraints of their social environments limited the perceptions of those who wrote the scriptures. Therefore, they could only articulate God within the confines of this limited comprehension. Consequently, today we express God as a man with human features, characteristics, behaviors, attitudes, temperament, etc. Notwithstanding, does God's male gender automatically subject women to the power and will of men. Again, the Bible tends to refute the unequal allocation of power in a marriage when it states that husbands and wives should submit to each other.[33] It can only follow that men are more preoccupied with securing their status and supremacy over women than God is.

There are several other theories that attempt to justify male dominance. One of these assumptions is "child caring." This theory claims that because women are the natural child bearers, their standard position is to remain in the home. Moreover, home and family should be the wife's principal focus.[34] However, is the wife automatically inferior because she is able to have children? Feminist generally argue that the stresses associated with having a child far exceeds any physical trauma a man voluntarily experiences. They conclude that this is avid proof that women are stronger and more durable than men are. Still, what does the ability or inability to have children have to do with male dominance and power?

Another theory of male dominance supposes that because a man is essentially physically stronger than a woman is he should naturally rule over them.[35] The problem here is the preexisting gap between the strength and abilities of males and females is beginning to narrow. Over the last fifty years or so, because of the acceptance of female fitness and athleticism, women are evolving to be just as fast and strong as men are. In another fifty years, we may see natural female strength equal or eclipse that of men. With all of these things stated, does superior physical ability reflect one's leadership aptitude? In other words, stronger does not mean better. Greater physical power does not equate to superiority in a marriage.

I could go on elaborating on many other theories of male dominance and refuting each in a similar manner, but I am sure you get my point. If not, the point is that Nature does not ordain power in a relationship. Male dominance is not a natural phenomenon for humans. Further, it is not a marital right or a privilege. The significance of status and hierarchal control in a marriage should yield to equity and mutual regard.

A woman who desires to be treated like a queen reinforces the fact that she wants a man—her king—to rule over her. Therefore, if she wants him to be her head then she should embrace her position as the tail. Equality begins with rejecting the romantic ideas that, although sound good and make us feel even better, only reinforce the attitudes that promote inequitable marriages and relationships.

Marriage and Conflict:
Fight the Good Fight

"All married couples should learn the art of battle as they should learn the art of making love. Good battle is objective and honest—never vicious or cruel. Good battle is healthy and constructive, and brings to a marriage the principle of equal partnership."
Ann Landers

Many of us have come to believe that conflict in many forms is a natural element of marriage. Moreover, we feel that disputes are a common sign of a successful marriage. This may explain why we tolerate relationships filled with excessive problems and overall unhappiness. The marriagebrokers continually remind us that minor bumps in the road in our marriages are a fixed phenomenon. However, a rational look at the naturally problem-filled marriage institution reveals the contrary. Logically speaking, what is our motivation to make such a life-long commitment if misery is the prime byproduct of a so-called healthy marriage?

Most of us usually have positive expectations when we first get married. Notwithstanding, we still holdfast to the myth that over the course of the relationship, the good times will outweigh the bad times. This tipping of the scales in the favor of the upbeat periods aids in our patience with a long, non-rewarding marriage. Cementing couples into relationships when they are not genuinely satisfied, indeed, may be the sole function of the myth that conflict is a natural part of marriage.

It would seem that the only non-sporting social arena where we ignore and even expect verbal and at times physical conflict is in the institution of marriage. We can anticipate severe repercussions if we interact with our co-workers in the same manner as we do our spouse. Similarly, we treat strangers on the street with more patience and understanding. We frown on children at play who associate in a way that causes discord. We learn to avoid confrontation and potentially problem-filled situations like the plague. Yet, when it comes to our marriages, we encourage and even expect couples to not only endure conflict but also to sometimes initiate it under the veil of healthy communication. Consequently, we often confuse intense arguments with therapeutic interaction that somehow draws us closer to our partner. Strangely enough, these confrontations are supposed to temper and strengthen a marriage just as fire does steel.

Unfortunately, when we regard marital conflict as normal, we excuse ourselves from critically evaluating its exact causes. Usually, evaluation, regrettably, does not take place until the clashes have risen to a point where they become unbearable for one or both parties. By then, the marriage may be beyond salvation.

Problem-ridden marriages do not have to be ordinary occurrences. Generally, problematic issues arise because of two specific reasons. Firstly, troubles surface because of our egos as we relentlessly try to satisfy our deep drive to be right. For example, every argument that we engage in stems from our attempt to persuade someone to see things from our point of view. If they do not see things our way and they refuse to adjust their actions accordingly, conflict follows. It usually does not matter to us where we adopted our points of view or where our ideas of marriage originated. What matters most to us is that others acknowledge and conform to our position—hence, conflict.

Secondly, confrontations occur because, just like you, whomever you are at odds with believes that their way of thinking is significant and everyone should acknowledge and respect it. Therefore, if no one surrenders to the other's point of view problems will continue. Oddly enough, if one party abandons their position under the veil of compromise and they totally embrace the ideas of their partner, forsaking their own, then problems of a different sort may surface. For example, self-esteem issues may emerge the more an individual unwillingly submits to the wishes of others. Furthermore, problems involving passive aggression can stress a marriage where one or both parties may not fully ditch their ideas about what they want from the marriage, but only simulate conformity. As a result, they will usually harbor concealed resentment for their spouse and the marriage. Hidden bitterness commonly becomes evident when the discontented spouse temporarily or permanently suspends intimacy. Consequently, their passive aggression forces their better half to reevaluate the lack of equity in the marriage.[36]

It is apparent that misery loves company as the marriagebrokers continue to encourage us to suffer through a less than satisfying marriage. The marriagebrokers themselves may realize the natural hardships associated with matrimony. Still, they expect us to value and perceive the institution of marriage as a sacred bond that reigns superior to our personal happiness.

More often than not, marriages riddled with difficulty do not improve with time. Troubles usually increase exponentially whether we address or ignore them. This may primarily be due in part to the natural resistance to changes in our personalities, our basic beliefs, ideologies, and lifestyles. Moreover, we generally do not consider our personal viewpoints to be irregular. Therefore, we do not comprehend the value or necessity of change. Since both persons concerned have similar mindsets, problems persist.

Clearly, it is possible to have a relationship free of serious conflict. We can sidestep traditional issues many married couples encounter with a little soul-searching. The simplest way, I guess, to avoid confrontation in a marriage is for one or both people to submit always to the whims and wishes of the other. Subsequently, the more passive one party is in the marriage the less conflict they experience (Figure 5). This may be far-fetched in that many of us usually at some point in our relationships insist on getting our way. Nevertheless, troubles would evaporate if mutual surrender were the norm. However, this practice of mutual surrender is rare and can lead to unseen dilemmas that I discussed earlier. Moreover, marital inequity comes to light in instances where only one individual consistently abandons their personal hopes, dreams, and desires for their partner in the name of love.

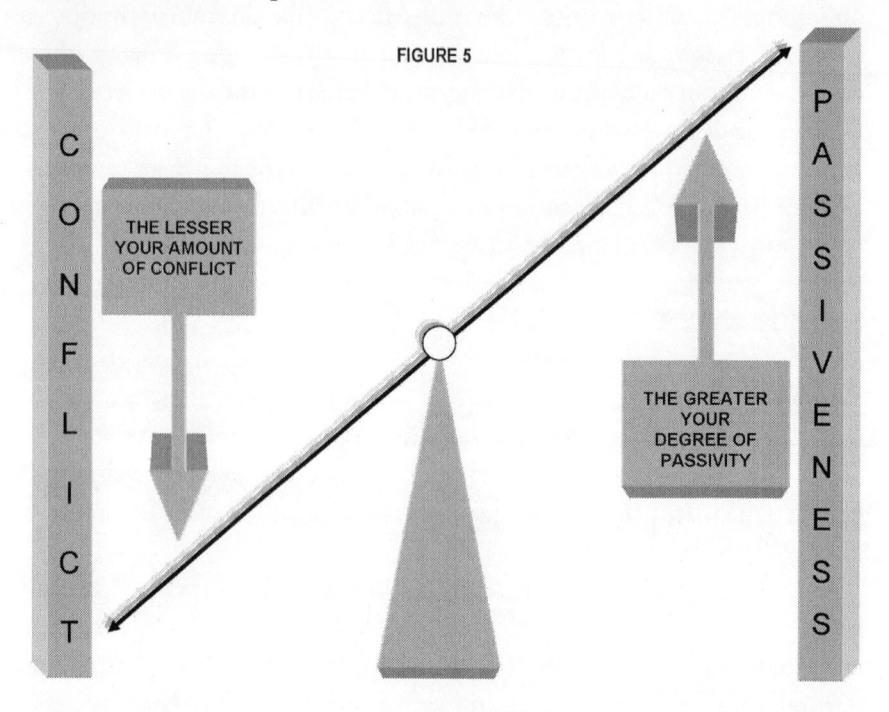

FIGURE 5

C O N F L I C T

THE LESSER YOUR AMOUNT OF CONFLICT

THE GREATER YOUR DEGREE OF PASSIVITY

P A S S I V E N E S S

We base, virtually all mutually agreed upon relationships on equity. Essentially, the very nature of marriage calls for it. Today, others view marriages that have one spouse benefiting and the other getting the short end of the deal as awkward and destined to fail. The more we feel that things are equal in relation to economics, domestic chores, responsibilities, maintenance, attention, love, etc. the happier we are with our marriage. In contrast, when we perceive inequality in these areas, our stress levels increase accordingly. The awareness of this added stress prompts us to employ various methods to bring stability back to the union. Some call these balancing tactics "power strategies."[37] I have included a list of the power strategies in Table 3. We bring into play one or more of these power tactics every time someone makes a decision and take certain actions that are contrary to our perceptions of what makes for an evenhanded relationship. We pout, yell, scream, make demands, cry, deny or increase intimacy, complain, nag, strike, seduce, whine, compliment, manipulate, insult, etc., etc., etc. until we successfully tip the scales back more towards the middle, if not in our favor. For this reason, we cannot avoid conflict as long as we continue to holdfast to our expectations of a balanced relationship. Subsequently, the more lopsided the marriage seems, the more disagreements we have.

Relationship Power Strategies*

Type of strategy	Example
Bullying	Threats, insults, ridicule, violence
Autocracy	Insisting, claiming greater knowledge, asserting authority
Manipulation	Dropping hints, flattery, seduction, reminding people what you have done for them
Supplication	Pleading, crying, acting ill, acting helpless
Bargaining	Reasoning, offering a compromise or trade-off
Disengagement	Sulking, trying to make one's partner feel guilty, leaving the scene
Asking	Ask for what you want
Laissez-faire	Do your own thing, just do it by yourself
Persistence	Repeatedly remind them what you want until they give in
Persuasion	Persuade them your way is right
Positive affect	Smile a lot, especially affectionate
Reasoning	Argue points logically
Stating importance	State how important it is to you
Talking	Talk about it, discuss differences
Telling	Tell them what you want, state your needs
Withdrawal	Clam up, become silent

Table 3

* I have used this table in the classroom for several years. The source of this table is undetermined.

There is also a risk that a spouse who always submits will become overly dependent. Eventually, their partner's aspirations eclipse and even swallow up their life, attitudes, personality, and dreams. Here too, conflict generally arises as one partner interprets the behaviors of the submissive spouse as needy, weak, or clingy. The non-submitting spouse sometimes takes actions to bring balance to the relationship by addressing their partner's neediness. They use power strategies like, suggesting, nagging, and complaining to persuade their spouse to seek independence. They do this without ever realizing that their initial desire to maintain the advantage in the relationship indirectly caused their partner's co-dependency.

Again, it is feasible to avoid conflict in a marriage if both parties understand the role of having high expectations and the utilization of power strategies play. For example, your spouse expects you to call them every time you deviate from your everyday, after work routine of coming straight home. If you fail to call, once you get home they may greet you with tears (supplication), the silent treatment (withdrawal), or a long dissertation (reasoning) concerning their required expectations. They are successful utilizing these techniques if they influence you to change your behavior and you call home from then on. However, you may avoid manipulation if you are already familiar with these methods and you realize that they are only using them to persuade you to meet their expectations.

Our high requirements and the use of various persuasive schemes eventually drain off the individuality, freedom, independence, and privacy rights from the relationship. Ironically, when this happens we can guarantee trouble. Difficulties follow when we realize that we have lost the core personal values, which form the foundation of self-worth. In other words, small differences, overtime, without doubt result in issues that are more serious as we realize we gradually sacrificed and devalued our personal desires and pleasures. To illustrate, one of my students told the class about the difficulties she was having at home with her parents, particularly her mother. This student (let us call her Sarah) was twenty years old, attending college, and had a decent job. Sarah explained to us how that even though she is an adult living at home with her parents, they still treat her like a child. Sarah has a ten o'clock weekday curfew, midnight on the weekends. If she turns off her cell phone or does not answer it for more than a couple of hours, her parents become overly and dramatically concerned. They tell her that they were worried that she was in an automobile accident or worse. Additionally, if Sarah fails to come home when expected her mother becomes extremely enraged. She told the class that her mother gets so angry that she often resorts to hitting her.

Clearly, in Sarah's situation, her parents, particularly her mother, are bullying Sarah into conforming to their demands. I told Sarah that she had a few choices. Her obvious choice is to remain in her present state of affairs and continue to suffer the loss of her individuality, freedom, and her privacy. Assuredly, if she goes on bowing down to her parent's wishes, conflict, in theory, should all but disappear. Unfortunately, although Sarah can avoid confrontation by making this choice, she risks the loss of her self-esteem and the personal confidence that typically comes along with independence.

Again, looking at Figure 5, the more passive she is when someone challenges her or her ideas the less chance Sarah has of generating conflict. However, she in turn gambles with her independence. Thus, the greater chance she has of a decreased sense of self-worth (Figures 6 and 7). In this instance, fear not love forms the foundation of Sarah's relationship with her parents. Moreover, it is fear that empowers most bullies.

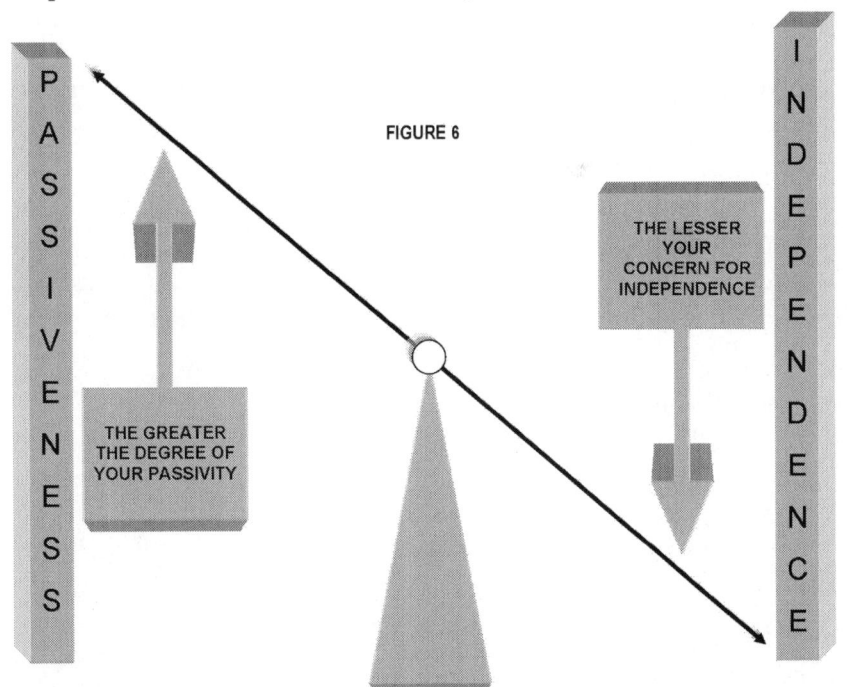

FIGURE 6

PASSIVENESS — THE GREATER THE DEGREE OF YOUR PASSIVITY

INDEPENDENCE — THE LESSER YOUR CONCERN FOR INDEPENDENCE

FIGURE 7

INDEPENDENCE

LOW SELF ESTEEM

THE LESSER YOUR CONCERN FOR INDEPENDENCE

THE GREATER YOUR DEGREE OF LOW SELF ESTEEM

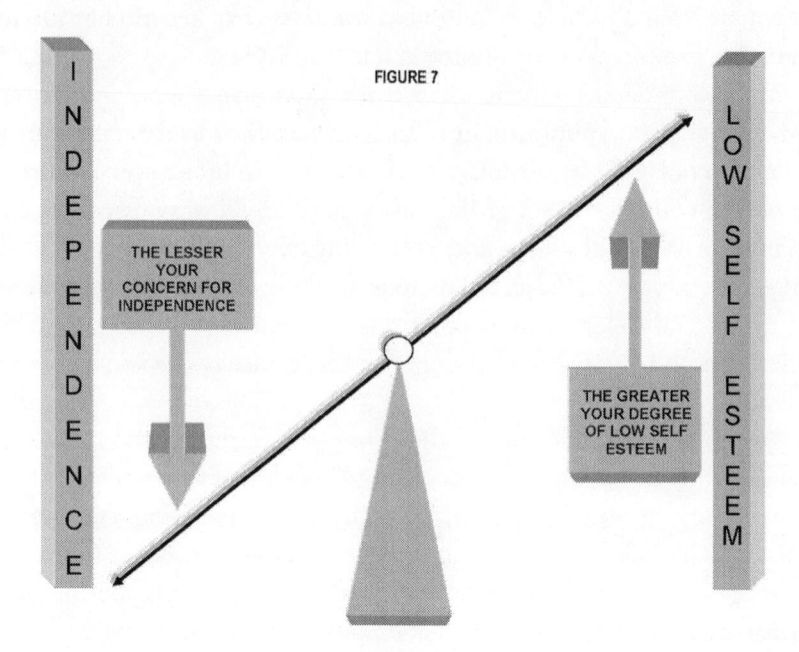

I told Sarah that she also has a second choice. This choice involves meeting the dilemma head-on—confronting conflict with conflict as it were. Let me make it clear that I was not suggesting initiating a physical altercation. Attempting to force your expectations on someone using physical force is not only childish and a sign of deeply rooted emotional issues, but it could land you in jail. I did, however, recommend to Sarah that she should not surrender to or ignore her tormentor, in this case her mother. Bullies usually use tactics like making insults, yelling, making threats, and violence to force someone into submission. I use the term bully here to describe those who use these more extreme power strategies to get their way. They interpret giving in or the ignoring of their behavior as signs of weakness. Persecutors respond to passive behavior like sharks to blood. They will continue to consume their victim until their prey totally breaks down or they force an altercation. I told Sarah that the only way she could hope to reduce or eliminate the conflict with her parents was to confront it—not with reason, passivity, patience, or violence, but by exposing the tyrants for who they are. I told her when her parents insisted on having their way with her affairs, that she must have the wherewithal to demand her independence and individuality as an adult. By the way, living under someone's roof does not justify giving up the rights to your personal freedom, especially as an adult. I went on to tell Sarah that when her parents employed the various power strategies I mentioned earlier, she was to deflate the affects of their behavior by standing her ground. I told the class that many times when we make a stand others threaten to leave us or put us out unless we conform to their demands. This particular power strategy falls under *disengagement*. If your loved ones threaten to leave when they do not get their way, let them go. Wholeheartedly support their decision. I have a pre-rehearsed response that I use when someone tries to persuade me by threatening to leave, it goes something like this—*Although it would hurt me deeply if you were to leave, please do not let me stand accused as the one who kept you from doing the very thing that you felt so compelled to do*. They then have only one of two choices to consider. Number one, they can make good on their threat and leave. Number two, they can back off trying to make me bow down to their demands and expectations. Either way I win. I told Sarah that if the bully resorted to emotional and/or physical abuse because she does not get her way, she should not only remove herself from the environment immediately, but she should not hesitate to call the police. Sarah is not a child who needs discipline. Sarah is an adult who deserves adult treatment. The laws that restrict people from assaulting other adults also bind Sarah's mom. I, personally, do not tolerate any assaults on my person or my property. I get the authorities involved immediately to let the bully know that I am serious about retaining my independence.

When I expressed this as a technique Sarah could use to deal with her situation at home, another student yelled out, "You're going to get her put out." I said, "Good…that would probably be the best thing for her at this point." Sarah's less passive behavior may generate more conflict, but in the end, she will regain her independence and as a byproduct heighten her sense of self-worth (Figures 8, 9, 10, 11, and 12).

FIGURE 8

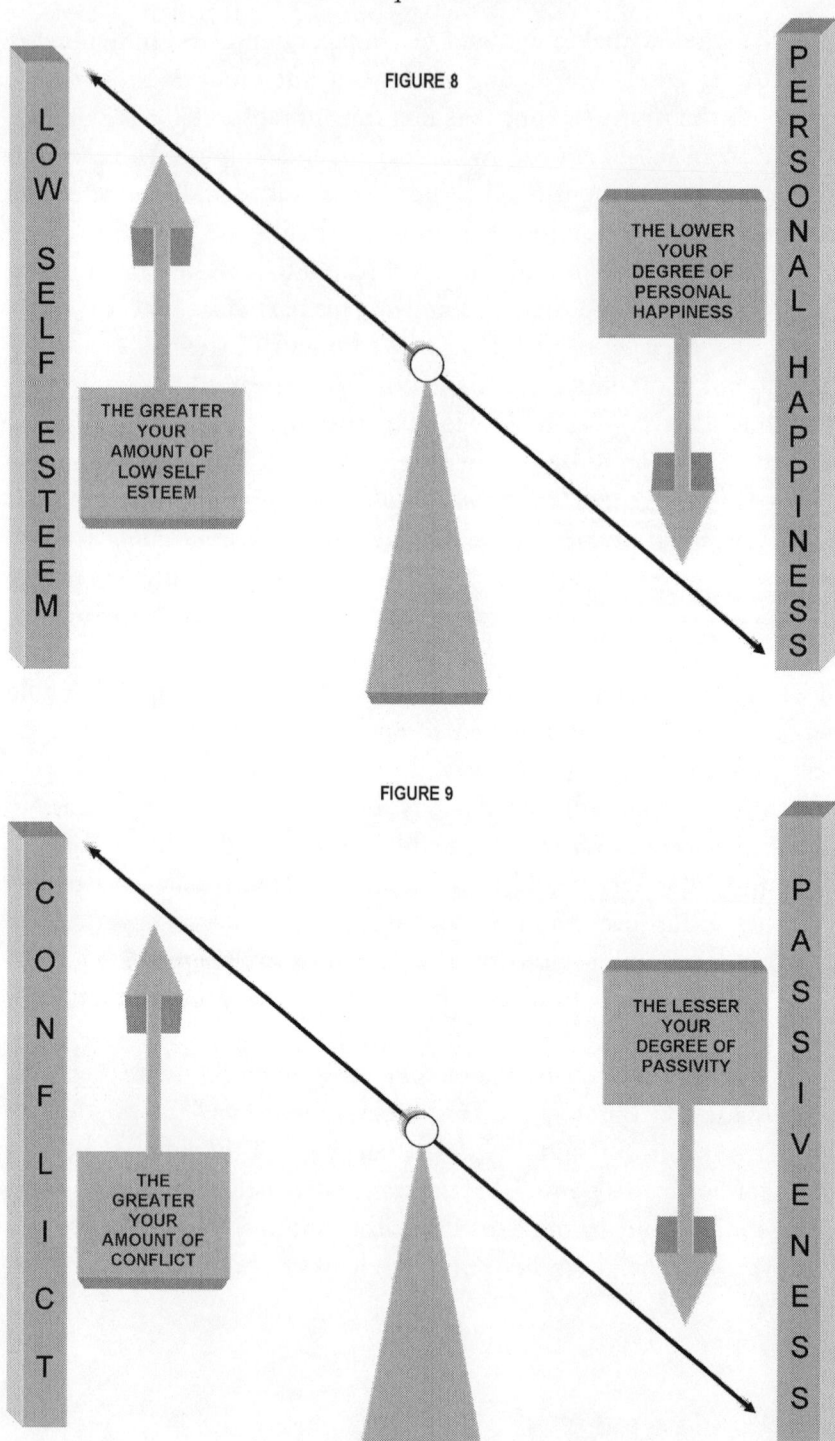

LOW SELF ESTEEM

THE GREATER YOUR AMOUNT OF LOW SELF ESTEEM

THE LOWER YOUR DEGREE OF PERSONAL HAPPINESS

PERSONAL HAPPINESS

FIGURE 9

CONFLICT

THE GREATER YOUR AMOUNT OF CONFLICT

THE LESSER YOUR DEGREE OF PASSIVITY

PASSIVENESS

Marriagebrokers

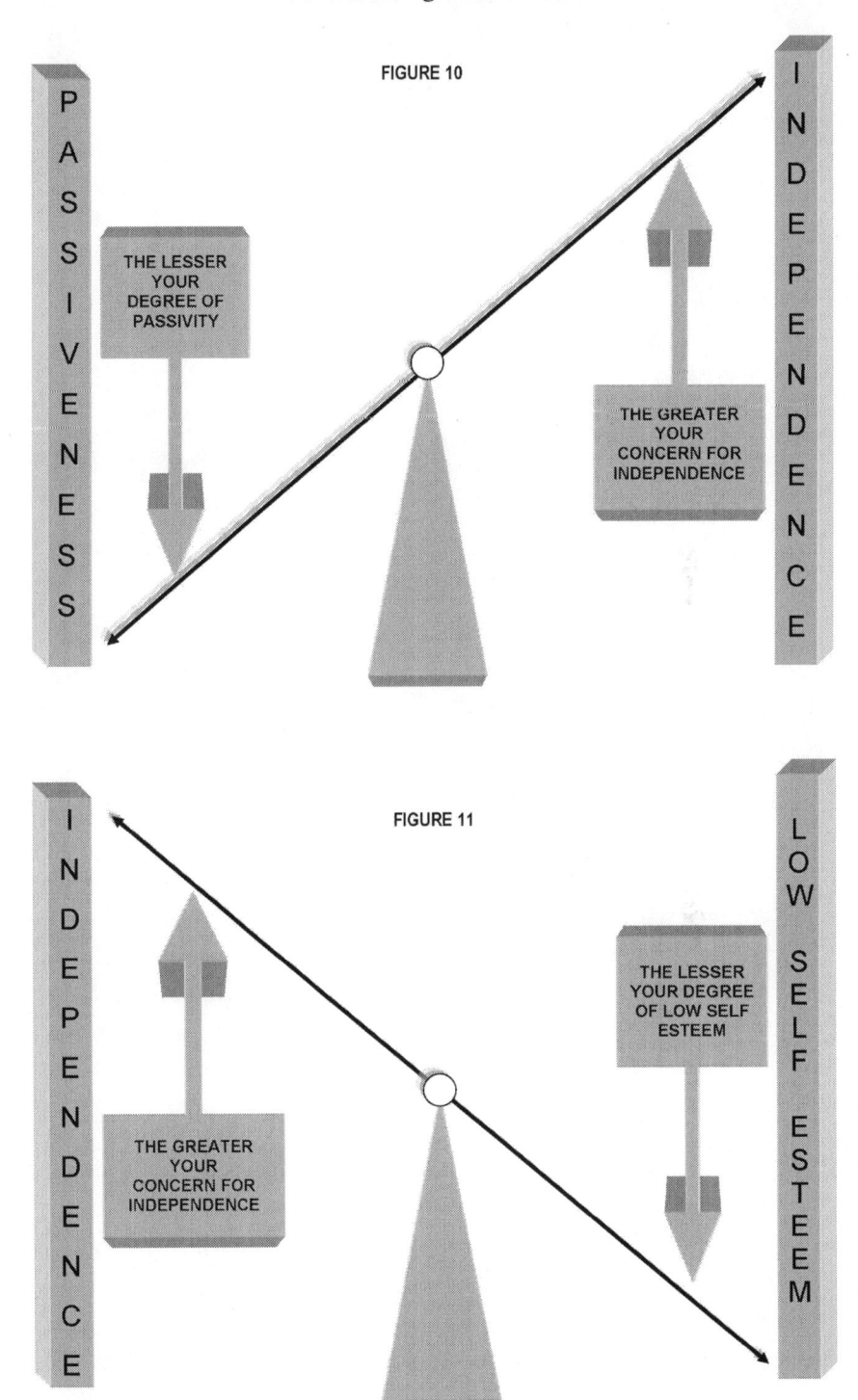

FIGURE 10

FIGURE 11

FIGURE 12

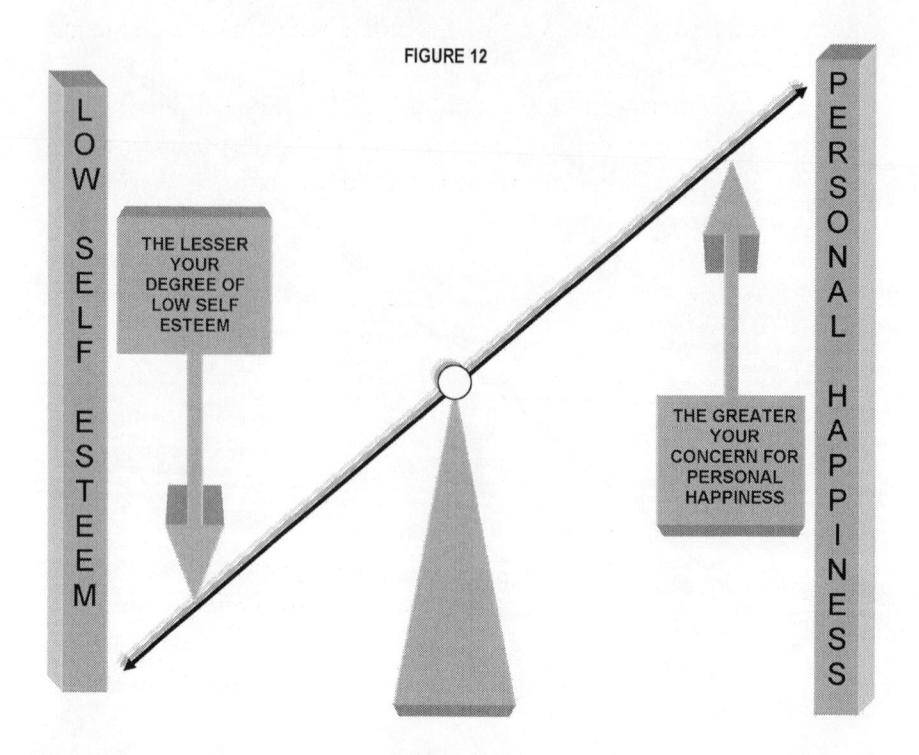

Balance diagram: LOW SELF ESTEEM on left (THE LESSER YOUR DEGREE OF LOW SELF ESTEEM) and PERSONAL HAPPINESS on right (THE GREATER YOUR CONCERN FOR PERSONAL HAPPINESS).

The less passive you are, the more you risk confrontation with those who try to persuade you to adopt their way of thinking. However, you eventually retain your independence. This sense of individuality prompts an increased level of self-esteem. Consequently, you become more content with your decisions and your life.

This brings me to Sarah's third option. Sarah should most definitely consider severing her current live-in relationship with her parents and learn to stand on her own. Gather her possessions and her composure and find a place of her own. Clearly, her actions will not be without consequence. No doubt, Sarah's parents will threaten to cut her off completely if she leaves. Nevertheless, her best option is to suffer disownment rather than suffer years of emotional castration by her parents. She will eventually be better off.

You can use Sarah's scenario in all of your relationships where you experience constant conflict. Your options are simple—1) stay and submit, 2) stay and stand your ground, or 3) leave. Dissolving the marriage is the best possible and maybe the only alternative in a relationship where ideologies are too far apart to be reconciled and where neither party can come to the point where they devalue the significance of their expectations.

Again, the marriagebrokers contend that we should preserve the sanctity of marriage despite the presence of lasting differences of opinion. They offer that one of the two (and that one usually refers to the wife) should submit to the other for the sake of peace in the home. I, on the other hand, assert that these pseudo-submissive gestures still lead to trouble down the line. I stress that if you lower your demands and expectations of the marriage and your spouse, you can eliminate most of your problems.

The root of all trouble found in all types of relationships are commonly found in the individual initiating the conflict. If you find that you have to resort to bullying, threatening, crying, fighting, manipulating, disengaging, nagging, complaining and so on to get what you want, simply modify your wants and satisfy your own desires. Do not continue to burden your spouse with the responsibility of satisfying your personal expectations. Only then will you begin to focus on the most essential part of your marriage—your spouse—for who they are and not for what they do for you.

Marriage and Divorce: *When to Let Go*

> *"There are two dilemmas that rattle the human skull:*
> *How do you hang on to someone who won't stay? And*
> *how do you get rid of someone who won't go?"*
> *The War of the Roses*
> Danny Devito

The marriagebrokers assert that marriage is a "death-do-you-part" venture. This outlook persists even though the divorce rate in this country remains comparably high. As I argued in Chapter 2, marriage is still one of the only agreements that we expect to last for a lifetime. Once more, we generally limit home purchases to 15, 20, or 30-year mortgage contracts. Even then, we anticipate breaking the contract after a few years and opening a new one on another property. There is no stigma attached to homeowners who sell their home and cash out the equity before the end of the initial period covered in the purchase agreement. Additionally, contracts associated with automobile purchases, furniture, timeshares, cell phones, and leases have only limited obligations. We can opt out by trade in or buying out of the deal. Major penalties do not result from our decision as long as we adhere to certain legal stipulations. This is not so with marriage. Unrelenting social pressure to conform to the norm cements us into lifeless marriages. We consider couples in our society who marry and who stay married to be normal—at least that is the expectation. Many of us, therefore, hope to meet these marital standards. As a result, our desire to conform exceeds our desire for individual achievement (Chapter 5).

Many married couples endure hardships because they believe that problems in a marriage are natural (Chapter 7). They, again accept as true that conflict, confusion, and chaos are actually a sign of a stable union. Therefore, instead of lowering their socially motivated expectations to stay married no matter what, they just minimize their need to be happy. Again, happiness, essentially, gives way to public acceptance.

I can only imagine the number of couples who would rush to the divorce courts if we finally erased the shame associated with divorce. Imagine telling your closest friends that you decided to end your marriage. What if they were excited about the news and jumped about jubilantly? Just think if you sent out hundreds of divorce announcements and people responded positively from around the country or the world. Imagine if everyone gathered around you to support your decision. What if they threw you a "bachelor again party" or an "unbridled shower"? No doubt, in these cases making up your mind to opt out of a bad marriage would be considerably easier.

Clearly, we find that the glue holding our marriages together has little to do with love. Undeniably, social pressure is the essential marital adhesive. If you are not yet convinced, just try this simple exercise. If you are married or in a long-term, co-habitation arrangement, merely visualize ending your relationship. The first person or thing that comes to your mind as the reason for not ending the relationship is probably the very thing behind your motivation to remain together. We often initially think, "what about the children." In this case, it is the children that hold your marriage together, not love. Sometimes we first consider how our family, close friends, neighbors or the church members will react to our decision. Indeed, our concern for public opinion influences our concern for our marital status in this instance.

Okay, with all of these things stated, let us return to the main topic of conversation in this chapter—when do we let go? Of course, there may be universal reasons that justify divorce in this country (I use the term universal loosely here in that many religious subcultures consistently encourage spouses, particularly the wife, to suffer through troubling issues. Many religions interpret marital chaos as simply the trying of your faith.[38] Consequently, the more you are able endure the difficulties associated with a troubled marriage, the better off you are and spiritually stronger you will be in the eyes of God. A preacher once quoted, "If you marry a lemon, just add sugar and make lemonade". Divorce, however, is not an acceptable option). Grounds for divorce usually include, but are not limited to, physical and/or emotional abuse, neglect, drug or alcohol addiction, etc. Individuals often endure marriages that exhibit one or more of these no-brainer reasons to divorce usually out of the fear of being alone. Women, because they have given up their right to share power in the marriage, often find it difficult to leave an abusive marriage. They have traded their careers and economic independence for the comfort of their domestic roles. Therefore, when problems intensify, some women have very few or no other options but to stay with their abusive husbands. As a result, they compromise their safety and often the safety of their children for the so-called security of marriage.

Additionally, society discourages men from leaving a marriage where the wife is abusive. Men tend to regard their egos over their well-being. Consequently, they will downplay problematic situations and put forth a front of success even though the marriage is in shambles.

We consider divorce to be the last of the last resort in marital problem solving. However, couples should immediately abandon a marriage that no longer provides a safe haven for their physical, emotional, or psychological welfare. In other words, if constant arguing and bickering is the norm for your marriage, then this negatively polluted atmosphere ceases to be beneficial for every person in the household. The marriagebrokers tell us that if we hang in there and if we learn to interpret the negatively charged atmosphere as a symbol of a healthy union then ultimate happiness and contentment will come—eventually. However, it is irrational to think that peace and harmony could result out of chaos and confusion. A fountain cannot gush out both bitter and sweet water.[39] There has to be some measure of residual emotional damage or physical consequence.

Arguments and fighting are signs of severe underlying problems. Couples must immediately address and attempt to resolve hidden issues.

These types of conflicts are not natural occurrences that we can use as indicators for gauging whether we have a healthy or a weak marriage.

Furthermore, our decision to abandon an unhealthy marriage would be easier if we practice regarding ourselves more highly than we regard other people's opinions of us. Once we realize that the wants, needs, and requirements of society concerning marriage have engulfed ours, it may be time to let go. Additionally, it may be time to dissolve your marriage if you find it difficult to distinguish between what makes you happy and what makes you look happy to others. Remember, you are the most important person in all of your relationships. This is because all of your intimate and non-intimate interactions begin and end with you. It only follows, that if you take care of your wants and needs and enhance your personal life first, you will in turn enhance the livelihood of your loved ones.

Again, if you have difficulty separating your personal happiness from the social expectations of happiness, be wary. In other words, if you can only achieve individual satisfaction when you perform your predetermined social and marital obligations, your happiness is not by individual choice. A joy exists outside of the social box (whatever the "box" is).

If we sacrifice ourselves for the sake of the whole, in this case, the whole means the family, the whole, subsequently, consumes us. We lose sight of our individuality and our personal goals as a result. The whole should not and cannot be more important than the sum of its parts. The parts, meaning the individual family members, make up and fortify the whole (I cover this concept in detail in the next chapter). It may be time to reconsider our marital choices when the roles and social expectations of the whole become more important than the role players do, or when the role players define their lives by their assigned tasks (see Chapter 5). Unfortunately, those who reconsider whether they should get married or stay married can expect a certain measure of ridicule from onlookers.

I know that even suggesting that someone should end a marriage, good or bad, for his or her personal gain seems radical. I also realize the fallout I will surely experience because of my position. Notwithstanding, when I rationally examine and begin to question the validity and relevance of the social practices we often take for granted, I cannot help but feel duped into believing that there is only one way to obtain social fulfillment. There are, undoubtedly, other socially satisfying perspectives, alternatives, and lifestyles available to us. Therefore, I do not introduce my arguments without realizing that they are neither right, nor are they wrong. My position on marriage is plainly different from the norm. The marriage practices that we undertake are apparently ineffective—that is if you judge marital affectivity by its historical lack of longevity as seen in the high divorce rate in this country. For that reason, we may finally need to take a different approach to marriage, at the very least question it. One approach should involve allowing spouses the opportunity to opt out of a bad marriage with the least possible amount of social ridicule.

Marriage and Me: Me, Myself, and We

"All the affectionate feelings of a man for others are an extension of his feelings for himself"
Aristotle

The marriagebrokers maintain that the family forms the foundation of a successful marriage. The term family implies a sense of *we-ness* as opposed to a *me-ness* mentality. Therefore, the marriagebrokers instill in members of society the importance of the sacredness of the family unit. The family consists of several distinctive individuals, all of whom should strive to promote harmony in the home. As I have mentioned in the previous chapters, we constantly sacrifice our personal desires for the necessities of the family. Consequently, family traditions and goals supersede individual needs or wants. To illustrate, how many times have you gotten into trouble because you put your priorities before the family? Try to remember the incidences where your loved ones scolded you for missing a traditional family event like Thanksgiving or Christmas dinner, a wedding, or grandma's birthday party. Your relatives, at times, may have temporarily stopped talking to you because you violated a family tradition.

Most of us have no problem with putting the family first because society programs us to interpret the family as the center point of our existence. It is difficult to argue the value of the family, however.

Its primary function is to replace and socialize members of society.[40] Additionally, several studies have concluded that to survive human beings, by nature, require a strong sense of social attachment.[41] Therefore, our society as we know it would not exist without the family. Families offer protection, identity, training, and is the central source of economic consumption.[42] Based on this, we clearly must give the family unit substantial weight in American culture even today. Subsequently, it is easy to see how our individualism becomes secondary to the family after we are married.

Still, the foundation of every family is the individual. It only follows that in order to cultivate and strengthen the family we have to concentrate on and attempt to fortify specific family members—first. Unfortunately, we often flip this notion around. We ignore and discourage individuality thus weakening the foundation of the family.

A rational look at marriage and the family, however, suggests that encouraging individual choice and happiness would be far more effective in solidifying the family unit. I believe that we must consider the Golden Rule of Selfishness attitude. For example, if your spouse enjoys going out with their friends on Friday nights. Instead of insisting that they sacrifice their time with their friends to spend with the family, you encourage them to go out and enjoy themselves. Additionally, they must support you when you participate in equally satisfying activities that do not include the family whenever you like. Each of you may possibly learn that the newfound freedom and individuality significantly lessens the stresses associated with most marriages. Additionally, you both may find an increase in your overall satisfaction with the marriage, thus strengthening it. It all begins when you encourage your partner to indulge in activities outside of the family and insist on similar treatment for yourself. Simply put, do unto others, not because they are special and deserve it, but because they will do unto you in return, hence, the me-centered marriage.

A me-centered marriage involves implementing a selfish way of thinking. In other words, gear all of your actions towards ultimately benefiting you. Happy people positively affect their relationships. When a husband and wife have healthy associations, hobbies, and interests beyond the family, they may be more satisfied with their lives. Consequently, they will not burden their spouse with the responsibility of making them happy. As a result, they minimize disappointment and conflict in the marriage. Each spouse takes on the task of his or her personal pleasure. Contented partners also promote their spouse's self-actualization because they know that they both will benefit in the end. Thus, the happier you are doing your own thing, the less unhappy you make your spouse.

Me-centered marriages tend to be free of the unimportant issues other relationships experience. The lack of pettiness for those practicing me-centered marriages results because they are so preoccupied with themselves and their personal interests that they do not have time to attempt to change or control the actions of their spouse. They take on an "if you're happy, I'm happy" approach to their marriage. Understand though, those in me-centered marriages are not only happy because their partner is happy, they are mainly satisfied because their spouse is not causing them discontentment.

Why do so many of us have issues with our spouses when they want to go out with their friends or engage in activities that they enjoy? The marriagebrokers have brainwashed us so that we feel married couples must do everything together. They discourage separate sources of enjoyment for married persons. Accordingly, many of us have given up associating with close friends or participating in our favorite pastime or hobbies just to satisfy the insecurities of our partner.

Some of us may have, at some point, threatened to leave, started arguments or fights, or cut off intimacy because our significant other decided to do something that made them happy without including us. At the same time, we claimed that we loved them. However, if we really love them as we allege, wouldn't we want to see them happy? Then why get upset when your spouse decides to hang out with their friends after work or even take a trip without you? Instead of throwing a tantrum whenever your partner wants to go out for a drink after work, offer to buy the first round and hand them twenty bucks. Make sure they tell their friends that the first round was on you. Not only will this act of generosity act as a symbol of your security with your marriage, but also your spouse will most likely return the favor when you want to indulge in your favorite pastime. We see that you were not understanding and kind strictly for your partner's benefit, but your actions were selfishly motivated. Clearly, both of you can gain from a me-centered mentality.

Take care of yourself first. Cultivate your skills. Indulge in your interests. Saturate yourself with selfishness. Encourage your partner to do the same. Eventually, you will find that your marriage will begin to strengthen as both of you begin to improve your talents and abilities, which, subsequently, leads to heightened self-esteem—hence, a more secure and happy union. Toss codependency out of the window forever.

For the one hundredth time—and this is definitely the central focus of this book—neither the marriage nor the family is more important than the individuals who make them up. Concentrate on the "me" and the "we" will become more obvious.

Although the me-centered approach to marriage sounds rational, others usually view it with skepticism. Whenever I suggest taking a selfish stance in a marriage, people frequently criticize my position and label me as negative and cynical. Notwithstanding, the pessimistic attitude towards marriage may serve a very useful purpose. Let me qualify my position by way of example. This revelation came to me one day as I rode my motorcycle on the 10 freeway in Southern California maneuvering through bumper-to-bumper traffic. I thought back when I initially took the motorcycle training course. The instructor constantly emphasized the notion of defensive riding. In other words, ride as if every other driver on the road is out to get you. As a result, when I ride I try to be constantly aware of my surroundings. I am especially attentive to other automobiles on the road. I always assume that the worse case scenario could happen at any time. To illustrate, the other day I was on my motorcycle traveling about 70 mph on the freeway. I noticed that about a half a mile ahead, traffic slowed abruptly. I assumed the car that was traveling just ahead of me in the lane to my right would suddenly pull into my lane without warning. That is exactly what it did. However, I had already played out the scenario in my mind. I planned to swerve into the emergency lane in case something happened. That is what I did, narrowly avoiding hitting him. I believe this method of preplanning, or thinking the worse saved me from severe injury or death that particular day. Whenever I come to an intersection, pass a driveway, or approach another vehicle, I always presume the worse and formulate an escape plan. I realize that no preplanning in the world can predict entirely the boneheaded actions of everyone, but I am sure it helps.

Again, we call this pessimistic type of thinking in relation to roadway management, defensive driving, and we encourage it. However, people discourage us from applying the same self-preserving outlook to our intimate relationships. They deem the defensive way of thinking to be negative and eventually detrimental to a marriage. I, on the other hand, argue that in order for us to avoid potential marital wrecks it is vital that we practice the same mental techniques as those who navigate the crowded roadways.

First, always anticipate the worse. Never expect your spouse to be perfect. They have shortcomings and faults just like you. Realize you cannot control the actions or inactions of others. However, you can adjust your attitudes and behaviors in preparation for the worse case scenario. Second, never assume that your partner is always paying attention to your needs or has your best interest at heart. Sometimes they get distracted and begin to drift off course.

Finally, learn to identify and predict bad behavior and annoying habits and have an escape plan. Many times, the same concerns that cause a marriage to end were prevalent early on in the relationship. However, we generally gloss over these problems with romanticism and optimism expecting love to work things out. Nevertheless, unaddressed issues only lead to major pile-ups. When we become skilled at "defensive dating," we will become proficient at avoiding most marital wrecks.

Even today, marriage remains one of the only areas in our life where people discourage suspicious investigation and label it as unnecessary worry. As I said before, when we invest in the stock market, purchase a home, choose a childcare provider, buy an automobile, acquire furniture, choose a school for our children, change careers, plan a vacation, or navigate the freeways everyone expects us to be skeptical and to count the costs before we make a final commitment. They call it wisdom when we exercise patience and make informed, practical decisions. Yet, when we employ the same skepticism and patience when choosing a life-long partner, they call it pessimism.

If negativism and pessimism helps us to sidestep severe wrecks in our relationships down the road, then we should value and cultivate this approach. However, I would rather be skeptical now, saving myself potential trouble as opposed to being blindly optimistic and risk suffering sure marital disaster. You decide what position is wiser; the marriagebrokers' perspective that preaches blind love and eternal happiness, or the me-centered defensive dating methodology that makes you attentive to the potholes and potential hazards common to most marriages, before it is too late.

Marriage or Me:
A Life Without Marriage

"Marriage is the triumph of imagination over intelligence."
Oscar Wilde

At some point during the social programming process that began as soon as we entered this world, social agents[43] implanted us with a deeply rooted drive to couple with someone else under the institution of marriage. We cannot exactly pinpoint where our intense desire to marry originated, yet the longing persists. During our childhood, particularly the adolescent years, many of us could not envision a life that did not include having a spouse and a family. As a child, we rehearsed our anticipated marital and familial roles through games such as playing house or playing with dolls and other toys.

Our marital and familial social programming is a slow, persistent, and formidable process. We have little or no say-so concerning the type of information society imparts to us. Additionally, we do not determine what to do with the social encoding once we receive it. Society has already mapped out our choices. Consequently, because society has predetermined our life's course, we tend to follow this life map without question.

Unfortunately, the social order teaches us that our value as a member of society remains well defined as long as we stay within socially accepted guidelines. If we make choices that conflict with our predetermined social programming, we experience what some call cognitive dissonance. Cognitive dissonance is the psychological stress we experience when our actions are contrary to our moral upbringing. We interpret this psychological discomfort, which usually comes in the form of guilt or embarrassment, as unhappiness. The more dissatisfied we are with our life, the greater our drive to reestablish the social connection with our loved ones. Hence, we drift back in line with our fixed social boundaries. As a result, we judge a life without marriage as failing and inadequate. This leads me back to the question of why we choose to marry. In lieu of the tremendous pressure placed upon us to marry someone, I use the word choose loosely. Is it actually free choice when we decide on a lifestyle that is not contrary to the social norm because we fear the negative reactions of those we respect the most? With all of these things stated, it is clear why we do not consider a life without marriage.

It appears that the only individuals comfortable with the idea of lifelong singlehood are those who have been previously married or those who rationally and critically weigh out the benefits and disadvantages of marriage. Some studies indicate that many married couples report a higher level of happiness compared to unmarried people.[44] Marriagebrokers use reports like these to encourage marriage. I, on the other hand, advocate achieving a high level of happiness without the aid of marriage. This unassisted contentment is necessary for emotional and psychological well being in the event the marriage breaks down. Many people suffer extreme emotional disappointment when their marriage ends in separation or divorce. However, if they were personally satisfied with life before marriage, the sorrowful affects of a deteriorating marriage would be less severe. Additionally, as I have previously stated, two emotionally healthy individuals who were completely content before the marriage only enhance the quality of a union. They do not stress the relationship by exerting unnecessary pressure on their partner to make them happy.

To illustrate, every semester I require each of my students to take themselves out on a date—alone. They cannot take any reading materials, their cell phones, or other forms of distractions. I am always puzzled at the number of students, both young and old, who have never been out to dinner or to a movie by themselves. Many report how uncomfortable, bored, or stupid they felt. I usually tell them that they are boring themselves to death. If you cannot keep yourself entertained, how can you be a good companion to someone else? If you do not like spending time with yourself, then who is going to enjoy spending time with you? We spend very little time getting pleasure from our own company.

Additionally, we constantly drown ourselves with information of some kind. Our environment relentlessly bombards us with all types of dialogue through television, radio, music, school, our jobs, billboards, and other people. However, we rarely take the time to process and analyze this information in a peaceful setting. Some of my best ideas come to me when I am alone in a quiet place free of outside interference.

Because of this experiment, several of my students realized how much they depend on others for personal fulfillment. Let me say again, to a certain degree many social scientists believe, myself included, that social attachments are essential for individual survival.[45] More clearly, no human being can continue to exist without some form of human contact. Nevertheless, survival and happiness are separate concepts. We can experience both survival and happiness outside of the institution of marriage. Someone who looks for others for fulfillment may cling more desperately to their partner eventually causing unnecessary conflict.

Concisely, I am saying that we can have a complete and satisfying life without being married. Without a doubt, there is nothing wrong with marriage. There may be, however, something wrong with believing that the only way we can feel whole is within the institution of marriage. The unrelenting social demands that, not so gently, nudge us in the direction of matrimony only promise a false sense of contentment. Yet, many married couples also report experiencing varying degrees of dissatisfaction with their lives.[46]

Henceforth, we should not consider unhappiness or loneliness as determining factors for deciding to get marriage. This begs the question of what should we consider to be an important and rational motive to marry. Most people instinctively list the following reasons for deciding to get married: they are in love, they want to start a family, they want to spend their life with only one individual, or they want a tax break. After closer analysis, we find that they can obtain each of these without being married.[47] Notwithstanding, we do not perceive these reasons for marriage as ultimately fulfilling without the social approval that usually comes via a public wedding ceremony.

So back to the issue at hand, why consider a life without marriage? Obviously, those who choose to remain single must fortify themselves against the unyielding criticism by those members of society who habitually conform to the norm. Frequently, many people sometimes accuse willing singles of being homosexual or promiscuous.[48] Nonetheless, if you desire to retain your personal rights to your privacy, freedom, and individuality, then you must take into account the choices that do not include conventional marriage.

Privacy, freedom, and individuality are only a few of the values we unwittingly surrender when we get married. Though we do not often profess it, there is an unspoken rule that we compromise these standards once we say, "I do." Many deny that it is possible or even appropriate to own another person. Yet, when we give up our rights to our privacy, freedom, and individuality, we indeed, commit ourselves to a relationship that reinforces the ownership mentality. We suppose marriages, where one partner maintains a life separate and private from their spouse, to be abnormal. Additionally, we expect decisions to go where you want, when you want, and how you want be done by consensus. Finally, individual identity becomes secondary to the "oneness" metaphor. We believe that after two distinct people marry they somehow become a single unit. They, as it were, miraculously develop a singleness of body, soul, and spirit—romantic, but very irrational. Essentially, those who relish, embrace, and romanticize the oneness of marriage have little problem denouncing their rights to individuality, especially when the alternative involves a lifestyle that falls outside of the social norm.

By now, you should have gathered that the foundation of this book lies in the cultivation of the self. Seemingly, the more you embrace the value of individual worth, the more difficult it will be for you to surrender to the social pressure to marry. It creates a contradiction in that the happier you are with being single, the more you qualify for a workable marital relationship. However, if you continue to value yourself, your freedom, your privacy, and your individuality, you will be less likely to commit to a union that naturally arrests these principles.

Marriagebrokers

Apparently, our only salvation to this dilemma is to base our decisions to marry or to remain single on various experimental studies. Some sociological surveys convey that married couples live longer, claim to be happier, and have more core values than unmarried people.[49] Even still, I have a problem with sacrificing my personal ideals for a few more days on this earth. Because without the core values of privacy, freedom, and individuality—which seem to be the very least we should expect as human beings—am I truly living?

Marriage and Tradition: *Some Creative Alternatives*

"Tradition is a guide, and not a jailer."
W. Somerset Maugham

It is highly unlikely that you will hear this from the marriagebrokers, but today there may be workable alternatives to traditional marriages. Though unconventional when compared to the norm, investigating other marital options may offer a solution to the problems familiar to today's intimate unions. Of course, there is the obvious choice to stay single, totally forsaking the notion of matrimony altogether. However, as we have discussed in the previous chapters, this option normally prompts severe, negative social restrictions. The unconventional choices that I am about to suggest may significantly minimize the effects of these penalties. Actually, they may allow those who make use of these marital alternatives the chance to experience a high level of social assimilation.

I hope that after you read this chapter, you will realize that I am not against marriage. I am only skeptical because of the negative results most traditional marriages produce. It may be that if you choose to employ any or all of these marriage alternatives, you may eventually experience a satisfying life with your significant other.

The Limited Term Marriage (LTM)

The first unconventional alternative is not my brainchild, but it may be a refreshing option. Limited term marriages (LTM's)[50] begin like traditional marriages. However, there is one significant twist. Instead of prospective couples entering into a marriage with high hopes of a long-term union, they mutually agree on a pre-designated duration period for the marriage. The LTM contains a clause that states after a few years—usually two or three—each spouse evaluates their degree of satisfaction with the marriage. Additionally, they critically analyze the performance or nonperformance of their partner. If after the agreed upon timetable, either spouse is discontented, they may opt out of the marriage without any negative repercussions. They do not have to go through a messy divorce. There is no ill will because the conditions of the marriage were predetermined. In this instance, they do not allow unrealistic expectations to get out of control.

Very seldom in LTM's do you see a case where someone begins to change for the worse. They realize that neither they nor their spouse is obligated to a long-standing commitment. Therefore, they usually will maintain the behaviors that originally attracted their partner to them to avoid an unsatisfactory evaluation. Everyone would always be on his or her best behavior, especially, the closer he or she comes to the assessment phase. An LTM would also be beneficial for those tired of being married, as they require no elaborate explanation of why they want out of the marriage.

What if your spouse had an annoying habit that you could not tolerate anymore? All you would need to do is purchase a gigantic wall calendar and mark the contract evaluation date in lipstick with a huge, bright red "X". Now, periodically post up in front of the calendar and simply smile without saying a word. Watch your spouse's annoying habit disappear like magic. Moreover, imagine the elation you would feel if you were in an unhappy LTM and the assessment period was approaching.

Even if you were happy with the marriage and decided to extend the contract, you could have a renewing of the contract ceremony every three years or so. All said the burdens associated with a life-long marriage commitment are nonexistent. An LTM affords spouses both the luxury of fulfilling their matrimonial obligation to society and the freedom of choice. They experience all of this without the hassle and stress of a traditional arrangement. LTM's may also motivate couples to stay together longer since they recognize they are in the relationship because they want to be and not because they have to be.

The Dutch Marriage (DM)

The Dutch marriage (DM) is based on a simple and uncomplicated premise. This principle involves both partners satisfying their own needs in the marriage, within reason. In other words, everyone shares equal financial and domestic responsibility. If one spouse has an issue in the relationship, it is their duty to take it upon themselves to rectify the problem. For example, if a husband wants to eat, he either cooks or goes out to get something. He does not burden his wife with the task of feeding him. Additionally, if the wife needs the oil changed in her car, she takes it to a mechanic. She does not wait for her husband to do it for her. If one partner likes the house neat, they clean it up or hire a maid. If someone wants flowers for Valentine's Day, they buy them. Each spouse also purchases their own Christmas and birthday gifts, if that is what they desire. The burden of marital satisfaction lies entirely with each individual in the DM.

The purpose of the DM is predominantly for sexual and social gratification. "You do you, I'll do me, and occasionally we will come together and do one another," forms the foundation of the DM. The advantage of the DM is that it greatly minimizes the expectations that traditional marriages encounter. In theory, the fewer the marital requirements we have, the fewer the marital disappointments.

The DM also fulfills our social obligation to marry. Other family members will no longer ridicule or pressure individuals at family functions to marry who are in a DM agreement. However, those who practice this type of marriage arrangement risk receiving minor criticism because of their independent mentality. Still, the DM offers an alternative to traditional customs and may afford married couples the happiness and independence they seek.

The Bi-local Marriage (BLM)

The next alternative to the conventional marriage arrangement is the bi-local marriage (BLM). In this type of marriage, both parties live in separate homes, states, or countries. The BLM could be workable in that it helps spouses to side step the everyday problems that cause many marriages to breakdown. No arguments or fights among spouses. Just peaceful, living apart from one another. I know that some of you have difficulty with the BLM situation because, again, the marriagebrokers have tried to convince us that marital problems and conflicts are indicators of a strong relationship. I guess if arguments and fights are signs of a healthy marriage, then peace and tranquility are symptoms of a troubled one. Anyway, a BLM helps us avoid the potential drama the marriagebrokers have told us to "look forward to."

There is no need to bicker about petty matters such as leaving the toilet seat up, not washing the dishes, overflowing garbage cans, unkempt houses, non-manicured lawns, someone coming home late or not at all, wild episodes of flatulence, menstrual cycles, etc. If you do not like the present situation, simply go to your own home and have it your way. Petty concerns disappear.

Of course, in a BLM, there is considerable chance that onlookers will be skeptical and critical of the unconventional arrangement. It is not normal for married couples to live voluntarily apart. However, you can merely explain the benefits of the BLM to your critics. Two homes mean twice the equity and subsequently twice the return on your investment.

The Fake Marriage (FM)

The final unconventional marriage option is my favorite. I call it the fake marriage (FM). The FM offers spouses much-desired social acceptance. In this type of marriage, both parties mutually agree to fabricate an elaborate wedding ceremony and unofficial marriage. No one except them knows that the arrangement is purely for show. Just like real weddings, they send out formal wedding announcements. They invite all of their close friends and relatives. The couple goes through all of the prenuptial and postnuptial rituals.

They have an official priest or minister preside over the ceremony. However, they do not file the necessary paperwork with the county office, therefore, voiding the marriage.

Months, even years pass. The pseudo-married couple receives the accolades from everyone witnessing the so-called marriage, as long as they do not reveal their secret. Whenever anyone asks them how their marriage is going, they just look at each other, smile, giggle and say, "Great, our marriage has never been better." Everyone would think, "Wow, what a happy couple...they've been together for years and they still get all bubbly around one another."

As with the other marriage options the fake marriage satisfies your social marital expectation—at least on the surface. By having a fake marriage, you now become part of the in-crowd. You also escape the embarrassment of being single while at the same time remaining unattached—sweet.

Understand that these creative alternatives to marriage are merely suggestions that differ from what we are accustomed to (Table 4). I clearly recognize that you can introduce a wealth of opposition that you feel shoot holes in each of these examples. Nevertheless, in your haste to dismiss them, make sure you are just as enthusiastic in honestly and rationally evaluating your motivation to follow without question the present marital traditions. Just because the manner in which we think about love and marriage is the only way we know or the only system society has taught us, it does not mean that those customs are right or the most effective. Furthermore, it does not mean that it is the solitary method for achieving personal and social actualization. Many argue, but few take the time to think objectively through the social institutions and their processes and formulate workable alternatives. They only criticize the untraditional perspectives. They often ask, "If we are going to practice a Dutch, limited term, bi-local, or fake marriage, what is the purpose of getting married?" I tell them that that is exactly the same question they should ask themselves before they undertake a traditional marriage.

The Pros and Cons of Creative Marriages

Type of Marriage	Pros	Cons
Limited Term Marriage (LTM)	Spouses are on their best behavior Sense of freedom Renewing of contract every three years	Must sign a prenuptial agreement Formal divorce proceedings Risk of public criticism if contract is not renewed
Dutch Marriage (DM)	Retain the rights to your property Lower expectations Fewer conflicts Socially acceptable Greater independence	Lack of romance Must sign a prenuptial agreement
Bi-Local Marriage (BLM)	Less opportunities for conflict Optimum independence Twice as much property	More expensive Less socially acceptable Increased opportunity for infidelity
Fake Marriage (FM)	Couple remains single High social acceptance Sense of freedom Retain the rights to your property More fun	Must maintain secrecy Children may find out

Table 4

Marriage and the Future: *Is Marriage Obsolete?*

"Contemporary man has rationalized the myths, but he has not been able to destroy them."
Octavio Paz

If we judge the significance of marriage in relation to its social functions, we may determine that marriage is less relevant today than ever before. Clearly, the primary social functions of marriage today include child bearing and rearing, economic support, emotional satisfaction, sexual gratification, love declaration, social legitimacy, social identity, and moral obligation. However, today we can meet many of these social tasks outside of the marital institution. Further, there appears to be considerably less of a stigma associated with those who choose to remain single.

An increasingly large number of people are opting to bear and rear their children in a one-parent household. They generally take on the task of parenthood willingly. Additionally, they openly share their parenting experience with others with pride as opposed to humiliation. Further, countless studies confirm that children who grow up in one and two-parent homes fair no differently in respect to intelligence, vocational success, and emotional well-being.[51] Hence, we find that procreation and the replenishing of the world's population can take place without matrimony.

Additionally, we can also more easily attain economic independence without being married today. We no longer have to pool our economic resources to survive. Furthermore, if a couple really needs to depend on one another for monetary support, they can just move in together. Although, society does not fully condone cohabitation, the dishonor associated with shacking up is diminishing.

Clearly, moral obligation, social identity and legitimization are the principal motivators for marriage in many cultures. All of them appear seamlessly intertwined. We become conscious of our moral obligations when others take note of and approve of our actions. Not only must they approve, but also they must give positive verbal and nonverbal feedback. Their endorsement encourages us to take part in essential social customs.

Notwithstanding, as the influences of religion and the church lessens its grip on the conscience of society, our primary motivators to marry become increasingly obsolete. Marriage, subsequently, is losing its validity as the gateway to God's favor. We therefore relegate the institution of marriage to a nostalgic social rite.

Often, when I ask people why they want to get married, their answers do not come easily—usually because they try to anticipate my response. Nevertheless, when they honestly appraise their marital intentions, they recognize its futility. When I speak of marital futility, I am talking about marriage's pointlessness in relation to personal happiness, emotional well-being, economic independence, social legitimization, moral obligation, family formulation, etc.

Our emotional and physical health, although I believe are grounded in our social attachment to others, need not be rooted in the matrimonial ideology. Unfortunately, many individuals do not self-actualize or feel a sense of worth if they fail to marry someone or if their marriage fails. Hence, for them, the act of marriage has become more vital than life. More so, the concept of marriage is their life.

Yet, a fulfilling life does exist outside of marriage. Self-actualization and fulfillment should develop regardless of our marital status. The marriagebrokers, over time, have caused us to interlace our perception of self-worth with our marital and family standing. I argue that we can achieve one without the other. Of course, others meet this stance with opposition because it is abnormal.

Again, when we critically think about why we get married today, we find our justifications insubstantial. Will the idea and the practice of marriage disappear from our culture? Not any time soon, I feel. However, in time we may experience an evolution or devolution of our attitudes towards marriage and the family.

The marriagebrokers are skeptical of the validity of the findings of those who take a rational look at marriage. The institution of marriage is only one of several socially generated ideologies society discourages us from questioning. It is a great deal more undemanding when we bring our attitudes and subsequent standard of living in line with the status quo. We, nonetheless, take for granted that the status quo is the only acceptable way of life. History, however, supports the fact that our so-called traditional attitudes towards marriage are a relatively new phenomenon.[52] Therefore, we can conclude that marriage and its social functions are not resistant to change as their meaning and uses tend to transform over time.

Again, because of this transformation we may not have to depend on marriage for protection, kinship bonds, social acceptance, etc. If this is so, then the question remains, "why marriage?" If this question provokes anxiety or frustration, then it warrants self-assessment. You, by now, should refuse to take the NIKE™ approach to making a long-term, life-changing decision based solely on myth and conjecture. It is imperative that we primarily base our choices on rational analysis.

Epilogue:
A Final Word

"Rough work, iconoclasm,[53] *but the only way to get at the truth."*
Oliver Wendell Holmes

So what of marriage? After all of my rhetoric, I understand that our beliefs, attitudes, and expectations will persist and even thrive. Romanticism and emotionalism are significantly more desirable than rationalism. The only good that comes from taking a critical look at life is the satisfaction of knowing the obvious.

I previously believed that our culture was evolving into a more logical society. The rapid technological advancements influenced my belief. However, I have concluded that these hi-tech strides have not led us down a logical path. Conversely, technology is transforming society into a people who are satisfied with hi-tech, informational machinery that performs our tasks and does our thinking for us. The marketers of various ideologies lull us into a relaxed state making us more susceptible to digesting their concepts.[54] Subsequently, we do not burden ourselves with the responsibility of analyzing and criticizing our beliefs, attitudes, or our behaviors. The technological elite and the marriagebrokers take care of all of this for us.

Those individuals who react and interact instinctively and emotionally within the established social system label those who question the obvious as strange, crazy, or deviant. The ability to explain the hows and whys, concerning marriage, is not as significant as the matrimonial act. Optimism drives our decisions and marital choices. We shun the evidence that conflicts with our preprogrammed dreams and aspirations. Additionally, we fear facing the reality of matrimonial insignificance.

Most of us center our entire existence on marriage and the family. It only follows that if someone forces us to analyze critically our marital choices we stand the chance of shattering our life-long dreams. Every time I lecture on the subject of intimate relationships, people instinctively deny my point of view. It is as though their duty is to protect the traditional ideas that they so rigorously adhere to. Still, the question of why we follow the marriagebrokers' lead so blindly constantly drives me. Moreover, why do people view me as a deviant when I probe the non-obvious aspects of everyday life, specifically marriage and romantic relationships? I must admit, sometimes I feel some regret when I speak with people who place a great deal of weight on marriage. I can at times see their frustration when their expectant vision of the future crumbles before their eyes.

I do not suppose that the ideas and concepts covered in this book are right, per se. I openly confess that I am definitely not a marriagebroker. I present that my ideas are not new, but simply different from popular opinion. I challenge everyone to take a step back and seriously think before you commit yourselves to a life-long marriage.

Again, let me reemphasize my position that there is nothing wrong with wanting to get married. I simply encourage you not to be afraid to go against the social grain. Clearly, the moral authorities have mapped out our life's course for us. Subsequently, we do not have to wrestle with the particulars of daily living. Our parents, grandparents, great grandparents, and great-great grandparents have religiously followed this way of life for decades, usually without question. I know you may say, "If it's good enough for them, it should be good enough for me." That may well be the case, but because people follow a particular custom or belief over a long period, that does not necessarily mean that it is right, true, or the most effective. Additionally, who is to say that their manner of living was good for them? There are workable models of thought and of living that go beyond what the marriagebrokers have exposed to us. Critically, examining these social alternatives may eventually allow you to experience the personal happiness and freedom most people desire—even in a marriage.

Why Get Married?

You do not marry for love; you can love without being married.
You do not marry to start a family; you can start a family without being married.
You do not marry to spend your life with someone; you can spend your life with them without being married.
You do not marry for commitment; you can commit without being married.
You should not marry because you are lonely; get a dog.
You should not marry to get a tax break; buy some land.
You should not marry for health benefits; get a job.
You should not marry because everyone expects you to; get a life.
So...why get married?

-anonymous

TIPS FOR A RATIONAL MARRIAGE

1) The marriage is more important than the wedding ceremony.

2) Spend the same amount of time, energy, and money preparing for the marriage as you do preparing for the wedding.

3) Couples hire "wedding planning" experts before the wedding, but they seldom consult "marriage planning" experts before the marriage.

4) Marriage is the only voluntary contract we enter into and expect to last a lifetime.

5) Don't treat your marriage like a NIKE™ commercial and "just do it"…Treat your marriage like an investment and "think through it".

6) Consider that there are no examples of a successful marriage in the Bible before you use it as a marital aid.

7) If you are only happy when you fulfill your marital role expectations, then it is not your happiness you experience, but everyone else's.

8) You are more important than the marriage…a family is not as important as the individuals who make it up.

9) You can never have both chivalry and equality in a marriage.

10) You are a real man because of your anatomical makeup, not because you cater to women.

11) You are a real woman because of your anatomical makeup, not because you cater to men.

12) If arguments and fights are signs of a healthy marriage, then peace and harmony are signs of an unhealthy one.

13) Whoever or whatever you think of first when you consider getting a divorce is what's holding your marriage together...not love.

14) Work on your strengths and not on strengthening the marriage... strong people make strong marriages.

15) There is life outside of marriage.

16) Up to 95% of the cultures in the world believe in having more than one spouse...maybe we got it wrong.

17) Jesus was single...so be God-like...stay single.

Notes

[1] Specifically, *The Thinker's Guide to Fallacies: The Art of Mental Trickery and Manipulation*, Dr. Richard Paul and Dr. Linda Elder, 2006.

[2] "Positive social sanctions" is a common Sociological term found in most introductory Social Science textbooks.

[3] *Marriage and Families: Changes, Choices, and Constraints*, Nijole V. Benokraitis, Prentice Hall, Upper Saddle River, NJ, 2005, p 261.

[4] *Marriage and Families: Changes, Choices, and Constraints*, Nijole V. Benokraitis, Prentice Hall, Upper Saddle River, NJ, 2005, p 261.

[5] Refer to my previous book, *Heartbrokers: A Rational Look at Romantic Love and Relationships*, Authorhouse Publishers, 2005. Specifically reference chapter 6, *Love and Expectations*.

[6] Religious marriagebrokers are those individuals in every culture who use religion to justify their expertise concerning marriage. I elaborate on the religious marriagebrokers in chapter 6.

[7] *Ways to the Center: An Introduction to World Religions*, 4th Edition, Denise L. Carmody and John T. Carmody, 1993.

[8] Emile Durkheim's writing on ceremonies and rituals in, *Consolatory Rhetoric: Grief, Symbol, and Ritual in the Greco-Roman Era (Studies in*

Rhetoric and Communication), Donovan J. Ochs, University of South Carolina Press, 1993.

[9] *Marriages and Families: Intimacy, Diversity, and Strengths*, 5th edition, David H. Olson and John Defrain, Mcgrall Hill, 2006, p 436.

[10] *Human Sexuality in a World of Diversity*, 6th edition, Jeffrey S. Nevid, Spencer and Lois Rathus, Pearson Publishers, 2005, page 23. Also reference *The Family*, 11th edition, J. Ross Eshleman and Richard A. Bulcroft, Pearson/Allyn and Bacon, 2006, p 18.

[11] *Human Sexuality in a World of Diversity*, 6th edition, Jeffrey S. Nevid, Spencer and Lois Rathus, Pearson Publishers, 2005, p 22.

[12] *Human Sexuality in a World of Diversity*, 6th edition, Jeffrey S. Nevid, Spencer and Lois Rathus, Pearson Publishers, 2005, p 24.

[13] *Human Sexuality in a World of Diversity*, 6th edition, Jeffrey S. Nevid, Spencer and Lois Rathus, Pearson Publishers, 2005, p 460.

[14] *Sexuality Now: Embracing Diversity*, Jannell L. Carroll, Thomson/Wadsworth Publishers, 2005, page 267. Also referred to as "serial marriage" in some texts, specifically, *Marriage and Family: The Quest for Intimacy*, 5th edition, Robert and Jeanette Lauer, McGraw Hill Publishers, 2004, p 409.

[15] *The Light of Conscience: How a Simple Act Can Change Your Life*, Bill Shore, Random House Publishing, 2004.

[16] Refer to my previous book, *Heartbrokers: A Rational Look at Romantic Love and Relationships*, Charles S. Fossett, III, Authorhouse Publishers, 2005, p xiv.

[17] *The Roots of Romanticism*, Isaiah Berlin, Princeton University Press, 1999, p 21.

[18] Genesis chapter 16, King James Version (KJV) of the Bible.

[19] Genesis chapter 29, KJV of the Bible.

[20] II Samuel chapter 11, KJV of the Bible.

[21] Judges chapters 14 and 16, KJV of the Bible.

[22] Exodus chapter 5, KJV of the Bible.

[23] I Kings chapter 11, KJV of the Bible.

[24] I Corinthians chapter 7, KJV of the Bible.

[25] Religious leaders who did not believe in the concept of the resurrection.

[26] Matthew chapter 22, KJV of the Bible.

[27] I Corinthians chapter 7 verse 28, KJV of the Bible.

[28] Proverbs chapter 21, KJV of the Bible.

[29] *Marriage, a History: How Love Conquered Marriage*, Stephanie Coontz, Penguin Books, 2005, p 6.

[30] A concept comprehensively outlined throughout the book entitled, *The Way We Never Were: American Families and the Nostalgia Trap*, Stephanie Coontz, Basic Books, 2000.

[31] *The Way We Never Were: American Families and the Nostalgia Trap*, Stephanie Coontz, Basic Books, 2000, p 43.

[32] Matthew chapter 22, KJV of the Bible.

[33] Ephesians chapter 5 verse 21, KJV of the Bible

[34] *Power and Society: An Introduction to the Social Sciences*, 8th edition, Thomas R. Dye, Hartcourt/Brace Publishers, 1999, p 58.

[35] *Power and Society: An Introduction to the Social Sciences*, 8th edition, Thomas R. Dye, Hartcourt/Brace Publishers, 1999, p 58.

[36] As referenced in a handout I have used in my classes for several years, that addresses "*equity theory.*" The original source of this information is undetermined.

[37] As referenced in a handout I have used in my classes for several years entitled, "*Men and Women Use Different Power Strategies.*" The original source of this information is undetermined.

[38] James chapter 1 verse 3, KJV of the Bible

[39] James chapter 3 verse 11, KJV of the Bible

[40] *Introduction to Sociology*, 8th edition, Henry L. Tischler, Thomson/Wadsworth, 2004, p 295.

[41] *Introduction to Sociology*, 8th edition, Henry L. Tischler, Thomson/Wadsworth, 2004, p 85.

[42] *Introduction to Sociology*, 8th edition, Henry L. Tischler, Thomson/Wadsworth, 2004, p 295.

[43] "A variety of agents, which also vary from culture to culture, are used to mold the child to fit into the society." *Introduction to Sociology*, 8th edition, Henry L. Tischler, Thomson/Wadsworth, 2004, p 92.

[44] *Human Sexuality in a World of Diversity*, 6th edition, Jeffrey S. Nevid, Spencer and Lois Rathus, Pearson Publishers, 2005, p 466.

[45] *Introduction to Sociology*, 8th edition, Henry L. Tischler, Thomson/Wadsworth, 2004, p 85.

[46] *Marriages and Families: Changes, Choices, and Constraints*, Benokraitis, Nijole, Pearson/Prentice Hall Publishers, 6th Edition, 2007, pp 295-296.

[47] Refer to my previous book, *Heartbrokers: A Rational Look at Romantic Love and Relationships*, Authorhouse Publishers, Charles S. Fossett, III, 2005, p 139.

[48] *Human Sexuality in a World of Diversity*, 6th edition, Jeffrey S. Nevid, Spencer and Lois Rathus, Pearson Publishers, 2005, p 459.

[49] Table, *The Benefits of Marriage and the Liabilities of Singlehood*, as referenced in *Choices in Relationships: An Introduction to Marriage and the Family*, 8th edition, Thomson/ Wadsworth Publishers, 2005, p 4.

[50] Referred to as the "time-limited marriage" in the article, *The Cure for Divorce*, Tad Low, *Men's Health Magazine*, July/August 2005, pp 108-112.

[51] *Marriage and Families: The Quest for Intimacy*, 5th edition, Robert and Jeanette Lauer, McGraw Hill Publishers, 2004, pp 28-34.

[52] *Marriage, a History: How Love Conquered Marriage*, Stephanie Coontz, Penquin Books, 2005, chapter 1, "The Radical Idea of Marrying for Love."

[53] The attacking of conventional beliefs or institutions. Webster's New Collegiate Dictionary.

[54] The basic premise of the book, *The Global Village: Transformations in World Life and Media in the 21st Century (Communication and Society)*, Marshall McCluhan, 1992, Oxford University Press.

About the Author

Charles has a Masters degree in Sociology and currently teaches marriage, family, and intimate relationship courses at California State University, Los Angeles. He recently published a book entitled, *Heartbrokers: A Rational Look at Romantic Love and Relationships*. He resides in Southern California with his two sons Chuckie and Stephen.

Made in the USA
Lexington, KY
16 December 2009